SRA

Writing and
Language Arts

Handbook

Level 2

Jean Wallace Gillet, Ed.D.
Reading Specialist
Orange County Public Schools
Orange County, Virginia

Charles Temple, Ph.D.
Professor of Education
Hobart and William Smith Colleges
Geneva, New York

James D. Williams, Ph.D.
Professor of Rhetoric and Linguistics
Director, University Writing Program
Soka University
California

SRA

Columbus, Ohio

The **McGraw-Hill** Companies

▶ Acknowledgments:

Grateful acknowledgment is given to the following publishers and copyright owners for permissions granted to reprint selections from their publications. All possible care has been taken to trace ownership and secure permission for each selection included.

From ALL EYES ON THE POND by Michael J. Rosen. Copyright © 1994 Michael Rosen. Reprinted by permission of Hyperion Books for Children.

From AMBER ON THE MOUNTAIN by Tony Johnston. Text copyright © 1994 by Tony Johnston. Used by permission of Dial Books for Young Readers, an imprint of Penguin Putnam Books for Young Readers, a division of Penguin Putnam, Inc.

From CINDERELLA, text copyright © 1977 by Charles Perrault. Reprinted with permission of Flammarion. All rights reserved.

From THE PAPER CRANE by Molly Bang. Text COPYRIGHT © 1985 BY MOLLY GARRET BANG. Used by permission of HarperCollins Publishers.

From STORY HOUR—STARRING MEGAN! text and illustrations © by Julie Brillhart. Reprinted by permission of the author.

From THE STORY OF THREE WHALES, text copyright © by Giles Whittell. Reproduced by permission of Candlewick Press, Inc., Cambridge, MA, on behalf of Walker Books Ltd., London.

From THE STORY OF THE STATUE OF LIBERTY by Betsy Maestro. TEXT COPYRIGHT © 1986 BY BETSY C. MAESTRO. Used by permission of HarperCollins Publishers.

www.sra4kids.com

▶ Table of Contents

You Are a Writer!

How do you describe yourself? You might tell how old you are. You may tell about your hobbies. You might talk about your favorite color or food. You could also say, "I'm a writer!"

You might think famous authors were born good writers. They worked hard to become good writers. No matter who you are, writing takes practice. The more you practice, the better your writing will be.

Why Should I Write?

Why should you write? Writing is a great way to share your feelings. Writing can also be fun. Here are some other reasons why people like to write.

"Writing helps me remember things."
—Kelly, age 8

"I love to share what I write with my class."
—Marcos, age 8

"Last week in the hall, I saw a sixth grader reading a poster I made!"
—Hani, age 8

How Can I Be a Writer?

Rosa never thought of herself as a writer. Then she began to think about the past week and made a list of all the kinds of writing she had done.

Take a Look

- my homework list
- my letter to Aunt Brenda
- my journal entry
- the birthday card I made for Dad
- the list of school supplies I need to buy
- a note to remember to get Jacob a present for his birthday party

Try It!

Think of the things you have written this week at home and at school. Make a list like Rosa's.

What Is a Writer?

Anyone who writes is a writer. To be a writer, you need a reason, or purpose, to write.

There are many purposes for writing. You may write lists to help yourself remember things. You might write in a diary or journal. You may write a note or a letter to a friend. You are a writer in school when you take notes in class.

There is no secret to being a writer. There are many ways to become a better writer.

Using This Handbook

Everyone is a writer, but writing isn't always easy. Every writer needs help gathering ideas and beginning to write. Good writers follow a process that helps them write better. You can make your writing better if you follow a similar process.

Athletes and musicians need to practice to be the best at what they do. To be a better writer, you will need to practice.

Now are you starting to picture yourself as a writer?

Fun Fact

The Pulitzer Prize is an award given to outstanding writers.

Traits of Good Writing

Good writing takes thought and practice. Writers aren't born good writers. This lesson will introduce you to some traits of good writing. These are helpful tips to help you in the writing process.

Ideas

▶ All good writing is clear and easy to read. Good writing also says something interesting. Good writing has many details, and it has correct facts.

Organization

▶ Good writing begins with a good opening. Information should be in order. Think about what readers need and want to know. Good writing presents the main idea in an interesting way.

Voice

▶ The writer's voice is his or her way of saying things. It helps the readers get to know the writer. A writer's personality comes through in writing with *voice*.

Word Choice

▶ A writer paints a picture with words. Good word choices make the writing interesting to read and easy to picture. Use words that help the reader see, feel, and hear your ideas, such as *sizzling* and *bumpy.* Use interesting verbs, such as *chuckled* and *crawled.*

Sentence Fluency

▶ Sentences in a paragraph should always stay on the topic. This helps the reader understand the paragraph.

Conventions

▶ Writing that has mistakes will confuse readers. Check for correct spelling, grammar, punctuation, and capitalization.

Presentation

▶ You should be proud of your work! Always make a clean and neat copy before anyone reads it. Add pictures or a drawing to make it look better. If you have a computer, try adding graphics or clip art. The way you present your work is very important.

Examples of Good Writing

These examples use the traits of good writing.

▶ **Ideas** "The Story of Three Whales" by Giles Whittell gives clear and interesting facts about whales.

> Humpback whales, Bowhead whales, and California Gray whales all come to the Arctic. In the summer of 1988, one particular herd of California Grays was plunging and rolling, leaping and belly-flopping off the north coast of Alaska.

▶ **Organization** "The Paper Crane" written by Molly Bang, shows good organization.

> A man once owned a restaurant on a busy road. He loved to cook good food and he loved to serve it. He worked from morning until night, and he was happy.
> But a new highway was built close by. Travelers drove straight from one place to another and no longer stopped at the restaurant. Many days went by when no guests came at all.

More Examples of Good Writing

▶ **Voice** Listen to the writer's voice of respect and wonder in "All Eyes on the Pond" by Michael J. Rosen.

> Here and there around this pond, countless eyes watch what goes on. Listen. They're all calling you:
> *Come closer; look! Come see my view.*

▶ **Word Choice** Tony Johnson uses clear words to describe a mountain in "Amber on the Mountain."

> Amber lived on a mountain so high, it poked through the clouds like a needle stuck in down. Trees bristled on it like porcupine quills.

▶ **Sentence Fluency** Julie Brillhart writes sentences that stay on the topic in "Story Hour—Starring Megan!"

> Megan liked the library because she had jobs to do. Her mother called her the "assistant." She put away the children's books and picked up the stuffed animals.

More Examples of Good Writing

▶ **Conventions** "Cinderella," retold by Fabio Coen, shows examples of correct spelling, capitalization, and punctuation.

> One day the King and Queen gave a ball. Cinderella helped her stepmother and her stepsisters to get ready. Then the three of them went to the ball. Cinderella was all alone. She began to cry. Suddenly her Fairy Godmother appeared.
> "Why are you crying?" she asked Cinderella.

▶ **Presentation** Jeff added photos to his poster on dinosaurs to make it more interesting to read.

> I like reading about dinosaurs.

Reading Your Writing

Using all of these traits will make your work clear and interesting. Your readers will understand and enjoy what you write.

Tips for Good Writing

Ideas
▶ Are your ideas interesting?

Organization
▶ Do you have an interesting opening?

▶ Are the events in the right order?

▶ Does your ending give readers things to consider?

Voice
▶ Did you say things in your own way?

Word Choice
▶ Did you paint a picture with your words?

Sentence Fluency
▶ Do your sentences stay on the topic?

Conventions
▶ Did you use capital letters for proper nouns, *I*, and at the beginning of each sentence?

▶ Have you checked for correct spellings?

▶ Did you use the right end mark after each sentence?

Presentation
▶ Did you make a clean and neat copy?

▶ Can you add pictures or clip art?

▶ Will your work look appealing to your readers?

The Writing Process

Learning to write can be fun. The writing process can help. There are five parts to the writing process: prewriting, drafting, revising, editing/proofreading, and publishing. You can use them to become a better writer.

The Writing Process

The writing process is a plan that anyone can follow. Each step will help you write clearly.

Prewriting

Prewriting is what you do before you start to write. Think about the kind of writing you are going to do. Decide on your topic. Make notes about what you want to say. Plan your writing.

Drafting

During this step, you write. Don't worry about making mistakes. Just get your ideas down on paper. Use your prewriting notes to help you.

1. Prewriting

2. Drafting

Revising

Reread your work. Will it make sense to readers? Can you add any details to make it clearer? Do you need to take out anything that doesn't belong? Should you put things in a different order?

Editing/Proofreading

Check your paper carefully and correct any mistakes in punctuation, capitalization, and spelling. Ask a classmate to help you look for mistakes in your work.

Publishing

The final step is to write or type on a computer a neat copy of your work. Then you can decide how to share it with others.

3. Revising

4. Editing/Proofreading

5. Publishing

Prewriting: Getting Started

If you were taking a long trip, you'd use a map and plan your trip before you leave. Writers plan their writing like travelers plan their trips.

Prewriting is an important part of the writing process. It is a plan for your writing.

What Kind of Writing?

What kind of writing do you need or want to do?

There are many kinds of writings you can do. Here are just a few:

- ▶ poems
- ▶ stories
- ▶ reports
- ▶ songs
- ▶ plays
- ▶ letters
- ▶ lists

Who Is Your Audience?

Your readers are your audience. Are you writing for other students in your class? Is it just for you? Is it for one special person? Once you know whom you are writing to, think about what your audience needs or wants to know.

What Is Your Purpose?

You need to think about your reason, or purpose, for writing. Are you writing to entertain your audience? Maybe you want to give your audience information about something. Perhaps your goal as a writer is to change someone's mind.

Looking for Ideas

There are many places to get ideas about what to write. Some writers keep a notebook. Just write down ideas whenever you get them.

Here are some ideas.

▶ things people say and do
▶ things you think about
▶ things you hear about in the news
▶ books you read
▶ things you can teach others
▶ things you learn in school
▶ things you do with your friends

Ruben loved reading the book *Charlotte's Web* by E. B. White. The book gave him a great writing idea. He is going to write about his pet hamster, Sam.

Choosing a Topic

Choose a topic that you know a lot about or that interests you. Think about your audience. What topic might be interesting or important to them?

Gathering Facts

Once you decide on your topic, you might need to learn more about it. The library is a good place to go for facts on a topic. You can use atlases and encyclopedias. You can also use the Internet to find some information. Talk to other people who know a lot about the topic. Make sure you gather facts about your topic. Stay focused on your topic, or your audience will get confused.

Ruben wants to learn more about hamsters. He borrowed two books from the library. He also looked up information on the Internet at school.

Planning Your Writing

The next step is to make notes about what you want to write. There are many ways to put your ideas together.

▶ list facts

▶ draw pictures

▶ make webs

▶ find out meanings of words you don't know

These notes are for you to use as you write.

Take a Look

Ruben decided to use a web to plan his writing.

Did Ruben's web have interesting information on hamsters? Did his notes stay on the topic? Do you think he has enough ideas for his writing?

Try It!

What are some topics or ideas you could use for writing? Choose something that interests you.

Reading Your Writing

Prewriting takes time, but it is one of the most important steps in writing. Without a plan your writing might not make sense to your audience. Also, your writing might be missing important ideas.

Fun Fact

A golden hamster can live as long as ten years.

Drafting: Beginning to Write

Now that you have planned your writing, it's time to write. Turn your notes into sentences. Write as much as you can. Use your notes, but if you think of something new, write it down. Don't worry about making mistakes. You can fix mistakes later.

Tips for Writing

▶ Write on one side of the paper, so you can cut it apart if you need to revise later.

▶ Leave space so you can add more later.

▶ Leave blanks when you don't know something.

▶ If you don't know how to spell a word, write the first letter and then as many other letters as you can.

Ruben used his web to plan a report about hamsters. It's not the way he wants it yet, but he has his ideas on paper.

Hamsters

They are soft and furry. They have short tails. Hamsters are easy to train and they make good pets. What do hamsters eat? They eat fruits, grain and vegetables. Hamsters carry their food in pouches. Everyone should get a hamster!

Reading Your Writing

Beginning to write will be easier if you remember to use your prewriting notes. Your notes or webs will help you put your ideas on paper. If you think of something new, always write that down, too.

Revising

You can make your writing better by changing parts of it. Making changes to improve your writing is called **revising.** Good writers use these tips when revising their work.

Tips for Good Writing

Ideas

▶ Is the main idea clear?

▶ Should any details be added?

▶ Is there any detail that isn't about the topic?

Organization

▶ Does my work have a beginning, a middle, and an end?

Sentence Fluency

▶ Do my sentences stay on the topic?

Word Choice

▶ Did I choose the best words to express my ideas?

Voice

▶ Will my audience want to keep reading?

Finally, compare your paper with your prewriting notes. Did you forget anything?

Ways to Fix Your Writing

Now make changes to your writing to be sure it says what you want it to say. Use these tips to revise your writing.

▶ Use arrows to move words and sentences.

▶ Use numbers to change the order of ideas.

▶ Cross out words or sentences that don't belong.

▶ Use scissors to cut apart the writing and use paste or tape to change the order of sentences or paragraphs.

▶ Use a caret (^) to put in new details or words.

Don't worry about misspellings or neatness when you revise. Focus on your ideas and how you express them.

Making Your Writing Clear

When you revise your writing, you need to make sure it is clearly written and makes sense. Be sure your ideas are written in the right order. To make your writing clear, ask yourself these questions.

Does my writing have

▶ an interesting beginning that tells the topic or main idea?

▶ a middle that gives important details about the topic or main idea?

▶ an ending that closes the writing in an interesting way?

▶ transition words such as *first, then, next,* and *finally,* that help the reader know which parts are the beginning, middle, and end?

After you answer these questions, you can make changes so your writing is easier to understand.

Below is Taylor's revision of a paragraph he wrote. See how he has marked his writing to put his ideas in order.

> There are lots of ways to make people smile. Smile at your classmates. In the morning, help fix breakfast. Leave your room neat. Put your toys away. Let a friend sit by the window on the bus. Say thank you when your teacher helps you with a math problem. These things will make people smile!

Fun Fact

It takes about 43 muscles in your face to frown but only about 17 muscles to smile. Keep smiling!

Try It!

Reread Taylor's work. How many places can you find where he can add words to make the order of the ideas clear?

Holding a Conference

A writer's conference is when you share your work with a teacher or classmates. They can help make your writing better.

What a Conference Looks Like

Every conference needs a writer and at least one listener. Sometimes there is a small group of three or four listeners.

Important Conference Rules

Every conference needs to follow important rules to make it helpful to the writer.

▶ Be polite.
▶ Listen carefully.
▶ Talk quietly and take turns speaking.
▶ Stay on the topic.

What the Writer Does

The writer has some important jobs to do to make the conference helpful.

1. Read the writing aloud. Practice reading before the conference.
2. Answer questions from the listeners.
3. Write down what the listeners say.

What the Listeners Do

The listeners also have important jobs to do to make the conference a success.

1. Listen quietly and carefully.
2. Show respect for the writer and the writing.
3. Ask questions about things you don't understand.
4. Tell what you like about the writing.
5. Make helpful suggestions that may make the writing better.

Taylor asked Terrell and Cindy to help him with his writing. He read to them. Here are their comments.

Terrell: I like that you told real things a person can do to help other people.

Cindy: You gave some good ideas for things to do at school.

Terrell: You could change your first sentence to a question to get people's attention.

Cindy: Maybe you could add more ways people can help their parents.

After the Conference

Taylor wrote what Cindy and Terrell said. Then he thanked them for their help. Next he will take their comments and decide what he is going to change. He will make changes to improve his writing.

Try It!

Did Taylor, Cindy, and Terrell follow all the rules about conferencing? Is there anything you would have done differently?

Reading Your Writing

Conferencing helps improve your writing. It helps you make sure that you are telling your audience what they need to know. It also helps you check that your work makes sense.

Editing/Proofreading

You have revised your writing so your ideas are clear and in the right order. Now it's time to read your writing to look for mistakes.

Here are some things to check.

- ▶ spelling
- ▶ punctuation
- ▶ capitalization

You can use a colored pencil, marker, or pen to mark these mistakes. You also will need a dictionary to help you with spelling.

Proofreading

Here are some proofreading marks to use to correct your work.

¶   Indent.

∧   Add something.

ℛ   Take out something.

☰   Make a capital letter.

/   Make a small letter.

sp   Check spelling.

⊙   Add a period.

Using Proofreading Marks

Use these marks in a different color to fix your paper quickly. Look carefully at the examples for each mark.

¶ **Begin a paragraph.**
¶It is the easiest sandwich to make. First you get the cheese, the bread, and the butter together.

∧ **Add words.**
Had the house been there for ∧ years?   *many*

✄ **Take out, or delete, words or punctuation.**
The dog ~~dog~~ ran away.

= **Change to a capital letter.**
<u>w</u>ashington, D.C., is the nation's capital.

/ **Change to a small letter.**
Harley hid behind the old /Tree.

sp **Check spelling; write the correct spelling above the word.**
Tad wore a green (cotten) sweater.   sp *cotton*

⊙ **Add a period.**
The dog ran quickly across the road⊙

Using an Editing/ Proofreading Checklist

Before you write or type a final, neat copy, use the checklist below. This will help you find mistakes. You can also ask a classmate to help you check. Don't forget to make your proofreading marks in a different color. Have a dictionary handy for you to use too.

▶ Does each sentence begin with a capital letter?

▶ Does each sentence end with the correct punctuation?

▶ Are any words missing, or are there any words that don't belong?

▶ Are words spelled correctly?

▶ Is each paragraph indented?

After you have checked your paper, you are ready to copy or type your paper neatly.

Using a Computer to Edit/Proofread

Most computers can check your spelling but be careful. The underlined word in the sentence below is not correct. The correct word is *their*. *There* is a real word, so a computer would not catch that mistake.

The children put <u>there</u> coats on the bed.

Computers are not just in a computer lab. There are computers in VCR's, digital watches, cars, and grocery store scanners.

Reading Your Writing

If you don't edit/proofread your work, mistakes keep the reader from understanding your ideas. You can use a checklist to help you correct your work.

Publishing Your Writing

Once you write or type a neat copy of your work, you may decide to share it with others. This sharing is called **publishing.**

Ways to Publish Your Writing

▶ Display it on a bulletin board.

▶ Put it in a class book.

▶ Read it aloud to the class.

▶ Perform it in front of an audience.

▶ Send it to a magazine or newspaper.

▶ Put the writing to music.

▶ Perform your writing for your class.

▶ Put on a puppet show or a play.

▶ Print a nice copy on the computer at school.

Sometimes you can work with other classmates to publish. Each student can do a different job to get ready for sharing. Be creative!

Getting Your Writing Ready to Publish

After you have fixed the mistakes, you can neatly handwrite or type your work. Before you do that, you need to think about how you want your finished work to look. This is called **presentation.**

Ideas for Presenting Your Writing

▶ kinds and colors of paper

▶ kinds and colors of pens or ink

▶ extra materials you might need for publishing, such as staples, yarn, and cloth for book covers

▶ drawings or photos

▶ charts, graphs, or tables

If you can use a computer, here are some ideas for publishing your writing.

▶ change the font color

▶ add graphics or clip art

Drawing Charts, Time Lines, and Graphs

There are many ways to present information in a visual way. Charts, time lines, and graphs are visual tools that help your audience see important information in a quick and easy way.

Drawings with Labels

Include drawings with labels that name important parts.

Charts

A chart is an easy way to show important information.

Jalisa's First Week of Summer Vacation

DAY	SUNDAY	MONDAY	TUESDAY	WEDNESDAY	THURSDAY	FRIDAY	SATURDAY
ACTIVITY	Fed the fish Went swimming	Fed the fish Read a book	Fed the fish Planted seeds	Fed the fish Went swimming	Fed the fish Helped make a pie	Fed the fish Went to the library	Fed the fish Cleaned my room

Time Lines

Time lines show the order in which events happened.

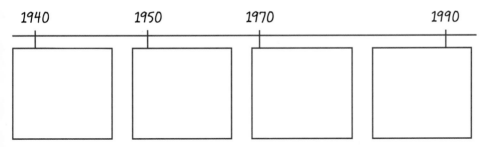

1940   1950   1970   1990

Circle Graph

This graph shows how a whole of something can be divided into parts.

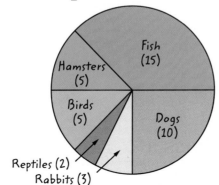

Fish (15)
Hamsters (5)
Birds (5)
Dogs (10)
Reptiles (2)
Rabbits (3)

Reading Your Writing

There are many ways to publish your writing. You can put it on display or share it with a friend. Drawings, charts, time lines, and graphs are other ways to publish your writing. Remember, how your work looks is important.

Keeping a Writing Portfolio

A **portfolio** is a place to keep your writing. You can include many different types of writing in your portfolio. In one part of your portfolio, you can keep your finished work.

A portfolio may contain

▶ stories
▶ poems
▶ letters
▶ reports
▶ comic strips
▶ plays
▶ reading journals
▶ songs

Keeping a portfolio is a good way for you, your teacher, and your family to see what you have learned as a writer. It is also fun to look back over work you have written.

Other Parts of Your Portfolio

You can label the different parts of your portfolio.

Writing Ideas

Good writers always keep ideas. Ideas can come from things that happen to you, books you read, talks with your friends, or things you learn in school. Not every idea will be used for writing.

Unfinished Writings

You may decide not to finish a writing. Don't throw it away. It doesn't matter whether it's prewriting notes or a revision. Keep it in your portfolio.

Special Words

Use one section of your portfolio to list special words. List words from units you study. Keep a list of words you learn and want to use. List words that you have trouble spelling.

Fun Fact

The word *publish* comes from a French word meaning "to make public."

Reading Your Writing

Your portfolio is a place that will show you and others how you've grown as a writer.

Following the Writing Process

Everyone in Maylee's second-grade class has to write a paragraph about something that happened to them over the summer.

Prewriting

First Maylee looked through the idea section of her writing portfolio for an idea. She found a good idea. She decided to tell about when her family got ready for a big storm.

Next Maylee thought about her audience. What would they need to know?

Then Maylee made notes to help her plan her paragraph. She put her notes in the order that things happened.

Take a Look

1. storm coming! → 2. borded up windows

3. take in lawn furniture → 4. shop for supplies

5. the storm hits

Writing a Draft

When Maylee finished planning her writing, she was ready to write. She used her notes as she wrote quickly. Maylee remembered not to worry about mistakes. She just worked on getting her ideas down.

Take a Look

A hurricane was coming in the ocean. Ocean water is salty. We had to hurry and get ready. We went to the store and got supplies. Dad put bords on all the windows. The windows had glass in them. The storm was over! I was glad we were ok.

Conferencing

Maylee's teacher asked Riley and Sara to listen as Maylee read to them. They listened quietly. Then Maylee wrote down what they said.

Riley: I like what you're writing. Hurricanes are exciting.

Sara: It was good you put important things to do to get ready for the storm.

Riley: I think you need an interesting or exciting first sentence to start your paragraph.

Sara: I think you have sentences that don't belong. You might take those out of your paragraph.

Riley: Your paragraph would be better if you added more details, like—what did you buy at the store?

Maylee thanked her two classmates. She thought they had good ideas about making her paragraph better.

Revising

Maylee reread her work carefully. Then she used some of the ideas from the conference to improve her work. She needed to make sure it was clear.

The Longest Nite

One day a hurricane was in the ocean not far from us. First my mom and I put the lawn furniture in the garadge. dad borded up the windows then we went to the store to by water candles bateries and flashlites. The wind was blowing so hard the trees bent over the ground. by morning the storm was over. I was glad no one in my family got hurt.

Try It!

Did Maylee make all the changes? Is there anything else you think she should change?

Editing/Proofreading

Maylee reread her work again. Now it has everything she wanted it to have. Next she needs to fix any mistakes in her writing. She will use a different color pencil and proofreading marks to mark the mistakes. She will do a final check using her editing checklist.

Take a Look

The Longest ~~Nite~~ *Night*

One day, a hurricane was in the ocean not far from us. First my mom and I put the lawn furniture in the ~~garadge~~ *garage*. dad ~~borded~~ *boarded* up the windows, then we went to the store to ~~by~~ *buy* water, candles, ~~bateries~~ *batteries* and ~~flashlites~~ *flashlights*. The wind was blowing so hard the trees bent over the ground, by morning the storm was over. I was glad no one in my family got hurt.

Publishing

Maylee wrote her paragraph neatly after she corrected the mistakes. She decided to draw pictures to show the important things that happened in her paragraph. Then she read her paragraph to the class. The pictures made it easy to see everything Maylee and her family did to get ready for the storm.

Take a Look

Here are the pictures that Maylee drew for her presentation.

Reading Your Writing

When you follow all of these steps, your writing will be interesting and will make sense to your readers.

Fun Fact

For a storm to be called a hurricane, its winds have to be over 72 miles per hour.

Forms of Writing

This is the part of the Handbook where you can find out how to write letters, reports, stories, descriptions, poetry, and much more. All the different kinds of writing you do are included here, plus some other kinds you may not have tried yet. Are you ready? Then let's get started.

Personal Writing

Do you make lists to remind yourself to do things?

Do you write notes to your friends?

These are examples of personal writing. Look at the next page for more kinds of personal writing you can do.

Lists

Lists help us remember things. Lists are clear and easy to read. When you write lists, use words or short phrases. You don't need to use sentences. Here are some different kinds of lists.

To-Do Lists

A list can help you remember to do different things. Number your list if there is an order to follow.

Take a Look

Rita is pet sitting for her neighbor. She lists the jobs she needs to do every day so she doesn't forget anything.

	1. feed fish, dog, cat, and bird
	2. take dog for a walk
	3. brush dog and cat
	4. give bird, cat, and dog water
	5. clean birdcage

Lists of Items

You can write lists of things you need to make a recipe, do a project, or buy at the store.

Take a Look

Mikala is going to make a treat to take to class for her birthday. She takes a shopping list to the store. It helps her get everything she needs.

- apples
- peanut butter
- chopped nuts
- napkins

Try It!

Think about a list you made lately. What kind of list was it? Who was the audience for your list?

Reading Your Writing

When you make a list, write only the words you need to remember. Don't write sentences.

Journals

A **journal** is a place of your own where you can write about all of the things that matter to you. Every day you think and do many things that you can write about in your journal.

Write in your journal every day. Write about what you see, hear, or think. It's fun to reread your journal later. It helps you remember important things. A journal is also a good place to find ideas for writing.

What to Write in Your Journal

There are no rules about what to put in your journal. Here are a few ideas.

▶ things you hear and see
▶ what you think
▶ what happens to you
▶ poems
▶ songs
▶ photos or drawings
▶ funny or interesting sayings
▶ jokes or funny stories
▶ lists of ideas for writing topics
▶ lists of words you like

Things to Remember

1. Write in your journal every day.

2. Write the date.

3. Don't worry about mistakes.

4. Write about different things.

5. Be creative.

6. It's your own writing place.

Take a Look

Here is a page from Neil's journal.

October 7--I brought my pet gerbil 'Roo to school today. The class liked to watch him eat. Taylee made a loud noise. 'Roo jumped out of the cage. We found him in the boy's bathroom. It took 10 of us to find him.

November 12--Don't forget to make my costume for the play. I'll need
- poster paper
- orange paint
- old t-shirt
- old pants

Learning Logs

A **learning log** is a kind of journal where you can keep a record of what you learn. You might keep a learning log about a science or a history project. You may want to keep a different log for each subject. You can also keep a learning log for many subjects.

Your learning log might have some or all of these things:

▶ notes
▶ questions
▶ charts
▶ pictures or drawings with labels
▶ your thoughts or ideas

Try It!

Can you think of a subject you are studying now for which you might make a learning log? What kinds of information could you include?

Take a Look

Rachel's class is studying butterflies for an Earth Day project. In this project, they are raising butterflies from eggs. The students will let the butterflies go after they can fly.

Rachel made a learning log to chart the changes. She filled in the chart as she watched her butterfly grow.

Date	Stage	What it looks like
March 3	Egg	Size of pin
March 13	Larva	Small of my finger tip
April 1	Larva	2 inches long black and yellow
April 12	Chrysalis	On a branch Hanging by thread In a green case
April 20	Butterfly	Breaks out Wings are soft and wrinkled Flew away

Notes and Cards

It's fun to write notes to friends or family. Sometimes you just want to tell about something that happened to you. Sometimes you might have a special reason for sending a note. When you send a note, make sure the reason for the note is clear and that your note is easy to read. Always remember to sign your name.

Cards

You may want to write your note on paper. Other times you might want to write your message in a card. You can make a drawing or put a picture on the front. People like to get cards. It makes them feel good.

Thank-You Notes

It's a nice thing to send a thank-you note or card when someone gives you a gift. You also can send a thank-you note if someone does something nice for you. Make sure you say why you are thanking the person.

Take a Look

Here's a thank-you note Tony wrote.

Dear Aunt Winnie,

Thank you for the great camera. I like taking pictures. I've taken 24 already. I will send some to you when I get them.

Love,
Tony

Get-Well Notes

Being sick is no fun. It makes you feel better when you get a card from someone. It helps to cheer you up. When you send cards to people who are sick, tell them you miss them. If you can, think of something funny to say or to draw to make them laugh.

Take a Look

Stevie misses his mom. Here is the get-well note he wrote to her.

Dear Mom,

I am sorry you are sick. I can't wait until you come home.

Love,

Stevie

Invitations

If you have a party, you will want to send an invitation.

Invitations tell
▶ who is giving the party
▶ the reason for the party
▶ the time of the party
▶ the date of the party
▶ where the party is taking place

Take a Look

Matt sent out this invitation.

Dear Mindy,   ◀ Greeting

    I am having a birthday party   ◀ Reason
on Friday, March 2, at 6:00 p.m.   ◀ When
The party is at my house. I live at
22 Willow Lane. Let me know if   ◀ Where
you can come. I hope you can!

Matt   ◀ Name

Friendly Letters

If you want to talk with friends or family who live nearby, you might walk to their house or call them on the telephone. When was the last time you talked to someone in another town or state?

What Is a Friendly Letter?

A **friendly letter** is a letter to a friend or relative. People like getting letters in the mail. A letter lets you think about what you really want to say. You can reread it and be sure it's just right.

E-mail is another type of a friendly letter. E-mail is just like writing a friendly letter, but your friend will get it faster. If you know someone with an e-mail address, try sending him or her a friendly e-mail.

Look at Sam's letter below. A friendly letter has five parts.

123 Rye Avenue
Millville, MN 73473
June 6, 2003 ◀ **Heading**

Dear Aunt Grace, ◀ **Greeting**

Guess what I got? Last week I ◀ **Body**
found a puppy hiding in the park.
He was all muddy. He was scared
and hungry. I took him home.
Dad and I fed him and gave him
a bath. We named him Patches.
Write back soon.

Love, ◀ **Closing**
Sam ◀ **Signature**

Getting Your Friendly Letter Ready to Mail

When you're done writing your letter, fold it into three parts so it fits into an envelope.

Addressing Your Envelope

▶ Write your name, street address, city, state, and zip code in the top left corner.

▶ Write the name and street address of the person you're sending the letter to in the middle.

▶ Use post office abbreviations for state names.

▶ Don't forget to put a stamp in the upper right corner.

Take a Look

Here's what Sam's envelope looks like.

Sam Burns
123 Rye Avenue ◀ **Your name**
Millville, MN 73473 **and address**

Stamp ▲

Mailing address ▶ Grace Martin
203 Bay Street
Southport, NC 28477

Tips for Writing a Friendly Letter

Prewriting Make a Plan

▶ Who will get your letter?

▶ What does that person want to know?

▶ Ask about the person's life.

▶ Tell about your friends and family.

Drafting Put Your Thoughts on Paper

▶ Use your notes to write a letter.

▶ Don't worry about mistakes. You can fix those later.

Revising Be Sure It Makes Sense

▶ **Ideas** Did you include everything you want to say?

▶ **Organization** Did you stay on the topic?

Editing/Proofreading Look Closely at Details

▶ **Conventions** Does your letter have all five parts? Are people's names capitalized? Are the greeting and closing followed by commas?

Publishing Sending Your Friendly Letter

▶ **Presentation** Write or type a neat copy of your letter. Get your envelope ready and mail your letter.

Business Letters

You write a **business letter** when you need something or if you have a problem. When you write a business letter, you are writing to a company or to a person you don't know.

When to Write a Business Letter

Here are some reasons to write a business letter:

▶ to order or ask for something
▶ to complain about a problem
▶ to ask for information about something
▶ to share your opinions or ideas about something

Try It!

Is there something you would like to order? Is there something you would like to know? If there is, you can write a business letter.

What to Say in Your Business Letter

What you say in your letter depends on your reason for writing. Keep in mind the person who will get your letter. He or she will be more willing to help if your letter is clear and polite.

Writing to Ask for Something

▶ Tell who you are.

▶ Tell exactly what you want.

▶ Tell why you want it.

▶ Thank the person for helping you.

Writing to Complain about Something

▶ Tell who you are.

▶ Tell exactly what the problem is.

▶ Tell how you feel about the problem.

▶ Tell what should be done to fix the problem.

▶ Thank the person for reading your letter.

Reading Your Writing

Make sure your letter is clearly written. The person reading your letter may be more likely to answer.

Parts of a Business Letter

A business letter has six parts.

Heading

▶ The heading is the sender's name and address plus the date.

Inside Address

▶ The inside address is the name and address of the person getting your letter.

Salutation or Greeting

▶ The salutation greets whom you are writing. A colon should follow the name.
  Dear Dr. Kirtley: Dear Ms. Adams:

▶ If you don't know the person's name, just write *Sir, Madam,* or the name of the company.

Body

▶ The body of the letter is where you tell about your problem or tell what you want to order.

Closing

▶ To end your letter, use one of these closings. Remember to use a comma.

  Yours truly,   Sincerely,   Thank you,

Signature

▶ Write your first and last name.

Read Kipper's letter asking a zoo owner for information about polar bears.

Heading ▶ 204 Laurel Drive
Oakmont, IL 50763
January 22, 2003

Inside Address ▶ Ms. Arnold
Wildwood Zoo
27 Highland Park Drive
Fairmont, IL 50721

Salutation ▶ Dear Ms. Arnold:

Body ▶ My name is Kipper Murphy. I am in second grade at Hills Elementary School. Our class will be studying animals of the Arctic. I am doing a report on polar bears. I know you have some polar bears in your zoo. You must know a lot about them.

Could you send me any information you have about polar bears? I want to learn as much as I can for my report.

Closing ▶ Thank you,

Signature ▶ Kipper Murphy

Sending Your Business Letter

When your letter is neatly typed or written, you are ready to send it.

Addressing Your Envelope

Neatly address your envelope by writing your name and address in the upper left corner of the envelope. Write the name and address of the person in the lower center of the envelope.

Tips for Addressing Your Envelope

▶ Capitalize all names of people, companies, streets, cities, and states.

▶ Use the post office abbreviations for state names.

▶ Use a comma between the city and state.

Kipper Murphy
204 Laurel Drive
Oakmont, IL 50763

Ms. Arnold
Wildwood Zoo
27 Highland Park Drive
Fairmont, IL 50721

▶ Don't forget to put a stamp in the top right corner of the envelope.

Folding Your Business Letter

Neatly fold your letter in three equal parts. Put your letter into the envelope. Seal the envelope and put a stamp on it. It's ready to drop in the mailbox!

Tips for Writing Business Letters

Prewriting Make a Plan

▶ Think about the reason for your letter. Make some notes.

▶ Who is going to get your letter?

Drafting Put Your Thoughts on Paper

▶ Use your notes to write the letter.

▶ Make sure you have all six parts of the letter.

Revising Be Sure It Makes Sense

▶ **Ideas** Did you describe your problem or what you need?

▶ **Voice** Is your letter polite?

▶ **Organization** Did you stay on the topic?

Editing/Proofreading Look Closely at the Details

▶ **Conventions** Capitalize names of people and places, the salutation, and the first word of the closing. Use a colon after the salutation. Use a comma after the closing.

Publishing Get Your Letter Ready to Mail

▶ **Presentation** Make sure your letter is neatly written or typed. Then put it in the envelope, stamp it, and seal it.

Expository Writing

Expository writing does two things. It explains how to do something, or it gives information about something.

Suppose you wrote a report about your favorite animal. Suppose you wrote directions explaining how to make your favorite sandwich. Both are examples of expository writing.

Writing a Summary

A **summary** paragraph tells the main idea and main points of a longer piece of writing. Read the following paragraphs from *The Story of the Statue of Liberty* by Betsy Maestro.

The Statue of Liberty stands on an island in New York Harbor. She is a beautiful sight to all who pass by her. Each year, millions of visitors ride the ferry out to the island. They climb to the top of the statue and enjoy the lovely view.

A young French sculptor named Frédéric Auguste Bartholdi visited America in 1871. When he saw Bedloe's Island in New York Harbor, he knew it was just the right place for a statue he wanted to build.

Bartholdi had created many other statues and monuments, but this one was to be very special. It was to be a present from the people of France to the people of America, as a remembrance of the old friendship between the two countries.

Summary Tips

▶ Always tell the main idea of each paragraph.
▶ The main idea is sometimes found near the beginning of each paragraph.
▶ Use your own words when you write a summary.
▶ Do not copy sentences from the paragraphs that you are summarizing.

Take a Look

Tory read the paragraphs about the Statue of Liberty. Then she wrote a summary of what she read.

> The Statue of Liberty is in the New York Harbor. Many people visit it every year. It was made by a French sculptor named Frédéric Auguste Bartholdi. It was a present from France to America.

Try It!

Can you think of anything Tory could add to her summary?

Giving Directions on How to Do Something

Sometimes you need to write directions for others. You will need to write clear directions so others can understand you.

Getting Ready to Write Directions

Planning is the most important step for this kind of writing. Think about all of the steps to do something. You need to make sure each step is in the right order. Also, think about your reader. Decide what your reader will need to know.

Take a Look

Nathan's friend Ben is keeping his dog for a week. Nathan wants Ben to give his dog a bath.

Fill the tub.

↓

Put dog in tub.

↓

Wash and rinse the dog.

↓

Take dog out and dry it.

Nathan used his notes to write directions for Ben on how to give the dog a bath.

How to Give a Dog a Bath

Here's how to give a dog a bath. First fill a tub with water. Make sure the water isn't too hot or too cold. Next put the dog in the tub. Then wash and rinse the dog. Finally take the dog out and dry him with a towel.

Try It!

Check Nathan's plan with his writing. Did he remember to put everything in? Did he add anything?

Reading Your Writing

To be sure your directions make sense, list everything that is needed before you start writing.

Giving Directions to a Place

Sometimes you may be asked to write directions on how to get to a certain place. Think about what your reader needs to know to get there.

Things to Remember

▶ Use location words such as *left* and *right*.

▶ Stick to what the reader needs to know. Adding information that is not important will only make it harder to follow your directions.

▶ Put your steps in the right order.

Take a Look

Lindy was asked to write directions to the playground for parents who are coming to the school's field day activities. Look at her prewriting web.

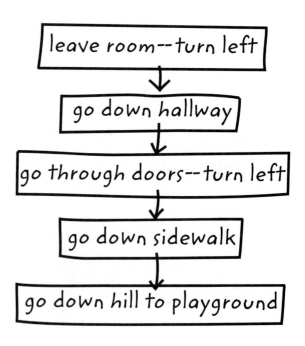

leave room--turn left

go down hallway

go through doors--turn left

go down sidewalk

go down hill to playground

Read Lindy's directions to the playground.

Getting to the Playground

1. Leave Mrs. Drake's classroom and turn left.
2. Go down the hallway past the library.
3. Go through the red double doors and turn left.
4. Walk down the sidewalk past the gym.
5. Go down the grassy hill to the playground.

Try It!

Did Lindy follow her plan? What details did she add to make her writing more interesting and clear?

Reading Your Writing

Did you tell your reader everything they need to know? If you leave something out, someone may get lost.

Tips for Writing How to Do Something

Prewriting | Make a Plan

▶ Picture the steps in your mind.

▶ Write your planning notes in order.

Drafting | Put Your Thoughts on Paper

▶ Keep your notes in front of you so you don't forget any steps.

▶ As you write, you may think of other steps or things the reader might need.

Revising | Be Sure It Makes Sense

▶ **Ideas** Did you forget any steps? Take out any information that isn't needed.

▶ **Organization** Is each step in the right order?

▶ **Word Choice** Make sure you use time and location words.

Editing/Proofreading | Look Closely at the Details

▶ **Conventions** Did you check the spelling?

Publishing | Share Your Work

▶ **Presentation** Neatly write or type your directions.

▶ Have someone try to follow your directions.

Tips for Writing How to Go Somewhere

Prewriting Make a Plan

▶ Think about where your reader needs to go.

▶ Start your directions from the place your reader is starting.

▶ Write your notes in the right order.

Drafting Put Your Thoughts on Paper

▶ Follow your notes carefully.

Revising Be Sure It Makes Sense

▶ **Ideas** Did you leave out any important details?

▶ **Organization** Are your steps in the right order?

▶ **Word Choice** Did you use place and location words?

Editing/Proofreading Look Closely at the Details

▶ **Conventions** Did you check the spelling?

Publishing Share Your Work

▶ **Presentation** Make a neatly written or typed copy.

▶ Draw a map for your reader.

Book Reviews

Writing a book review is a way to share a book you have read.

Writing a Fiction Book Review

Fiction is a story that is not true. Your fiction book review will have two parts.

1. what the book is about
2. how you feel about the book

Take a Look

Look at Mi's plan for her book review on the book *Corduroy* by Don Freeman.

What Happened:
  1. Corduroy lives in the store.
  2. Lisa wants to buy Corduroy.
  3. Lisa comes back and takes him home.

How I feel about the book
  1. fun to read
  2. makes me feel good

Mi used her plan to write her book review.

Corduroy

This book is about a toy bear that lives in a store. He wants someone to buy him and take him home. Lisa wants to buy him, but her mom won't let her. Then Lisa comes back and takes him home.

I think this book was fun to read. The end will make you feel warm and good.

Reading Your Writing

Make sure your readers get a good idea of what the book is about. You want them to read the book. Just don't tell too much or your readers will feel like they don't need to read the book.

Fun Fact

Teddy Bears are named after President Theodore (Teddy) Roosevelt.

Writing a Nonfiction Book Review

Nonfiction is writing about something that really happened.

Your book review will have two parts.

1. what the book is about

2. how you feel about the book

Here is Michael's plan for his book review.

What Happened:
1. 1770--Sequoyah was born
2. His other names: George Guess and Sogwali
3. wanted to make a written Cherokee alphabet

4. started on alphabet in 1809, finished in 1821
5. died in 1843

Michael used his plan to write his book review of the nonfiction book *Sequoyah: Inventor of the Cherokee Written Language.* Look at the two main parts of the review.

Sequoyah: Inventor of the Cherokee Written Language

This book is a true story of a famous Cherokee Native American. Sequoyah was born in 1770. He wished the Cherokee Native Americans had a written alphabet. He started working on one in 1809. He finished in 1821. Sequoyah died in 1843.

I really liked this book, and I think others will, too. It teaches about his life and how hard he worked. It shows that a person can do something great in life. I wish I could have met him.

Reading Your Writing

When you tell about a true story, make sure you tell about the most interesting parts so people will want to read the book.

Fun Fact

There are 85 characters, or letters, in the Cherokee alphabet and only 26 letters in the English alphabet.

Tips for Writing a Fiction Book Review

Prewriting Make a Plan

▶ Take notes about what happened.

Drafting Put Your Thoughts on Paper

▶ Write the title of the book and the author.

▶ Share the book's story.

▶ Tell how you feel about the book.

Revising Be Sure It Makes Sense

▶ **Ideas** What was the best part of the story? Don't give the ending away.

▶ **Organization** Are the events in order?

▶ **Voice** Does it sound like you like or dislike the book?

Editing/Proofreading Look Closely at the Details

▶ **Conventions** Check the spellings of names and places. Underline or italicize the title of the book.

Publishing Share Your Fiction Book Review

▶ **Presentation** Neatly write or type your book review. Share your review with your class.

Tips for Writing a Nonfiction Book Review

Prewriting **Make a Plan**

▶ Write down the book title.

▶ Think about how you feel about the book.

▶ Think about why other people might read the book.

Drafting **Put Your Thoughts on Paper**

▶ Tell that the story you read is true.

▶ Write about the important parts.

▶ Tell how you feel about the book and why.

Revising **Be Sure It Makes Sense**

▶ **Ideas** Take out parts that aren't important.

▶ **Organization** Make sure the facts are in the right order.

Editing/Proofreading **Look Closely at the Details**

▶ **Conventions** Capitalize all proper nouns. Underline or italicize the title of the book.

Publishing **Share Your Nonfiction Book Review**

▶ **Presentation** Neatly write or type your book review. Share your review with your classmates.

Reports

When you write a report, you need to think about these questions.

▶ What is going to be your topic?

▶ How are you going to learn about it?

▶ How are you going to write about it?

If you take one step at a time, you and your readers will enjoy finding out about your topic.

Choosing a Topic

Think about topics that interest you. After you choose a topic, make sure it isn't too big. For example, the topic of animals is too big and covers too much information. You should choose one kind of animal, such as whales, for your report.

Finding Information

You can look in many places to get information about your topic.

▶ books

▶ magazines

▶ encyclopedias

▶ people who know about the topic

▶ Internet at school

Taking Notes

As you find out about your topic, you will need to take notes. You will use them later when you write your report. There are many ways to take notes.

▶ note cards

▶ charts

▶ webs

Here's how to use a web to organize your notes. Write your topic in the bubble in the middle of the web. Then write a question you have about your topic in each outside bubble. Ask yourself two or three questions. Then add your facts around each question bubble.

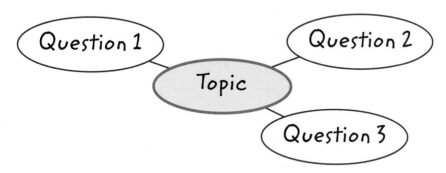

Katy used the web below to plan her report on whales. She chose what questions she wanted to answer. She used library books and magazines to find her answers. As she read about whales, she filled in the web with her notes.

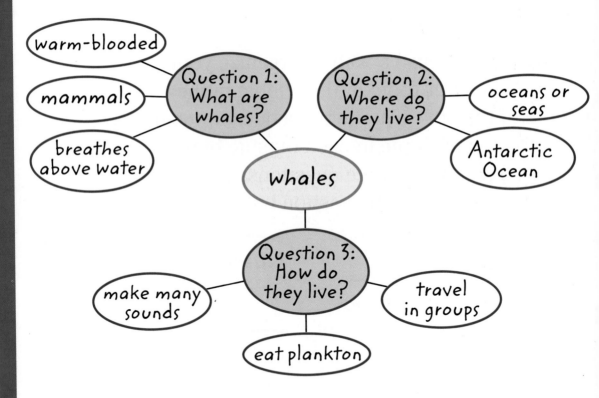

Katy used her notes to write her report on whales.

Whales

By Katy Floyd

What are whales? Whales are warm-blooded mammals. They need to come up to breathe the air above the water.

Where do whales live? They live in the water. They need water to hold their weight. Oceans and seas are the homes for whales. Many whales live in the Antarctic Ocean.

How do whales live? Many whales travel in groups. They make low sounds to talk to each other. They make high sounds to find food and to travel. They eat baby shrimp and plankton.

Fun Fact

The largest animal in the world is the blue whale, which can grow to over 100 feet long and weigh over 200 tons.

Tips for Writing a Report

Prewriting Make a Plan

▶ Choose the topic that interests you the most.

▶ Make sure your topic isn't too big.

▶ Ask yourself two questions about your topic.

▶ Use at least two sources to get your facts.

▶ Make notes using webs, charts, or note cards.

Drafting Put Your Thoughts on Paper

▶ Use your notes as you write your report.

Revising Be Sure It Makes Sense

▶ **Ideas** Did you put in all of your notes? Do you have any sentences or facts that don't belong?

▶ **Word Choice** Did you define hard words for your readers?

▶ **Organization** Are your facts in the right paragraphs?

▶ **Conventions** Check to be sure you have spelled any special words or names correctly.

▶ Make sure to indent each new paragraph.

▶ Don't forget to give your report a title.

▶ Capitalize any proper nouns and the main words in a title.

Publishing Share Your Report

▶ **Presentation** Neatly write or type a copy of your report.

▶ You may want to draw a picture or add photos to go with your report.

▶ You might share your report by reading it aloud to the class or to small groups of classmates.

Sheepherding in New Zealand by Jamie Wells

Narrative Writing

Narrative writing tells a story. The story can be true or make-believe. When you write a story, you are telling your readers what happened. Your story needs a beginning, a middle, and an end. It also needs a setting and characters. Look at the next page for some different kinds of stories you can write.

Personal Narratives

A **personal narrative** tells about something that has happened in your life.

Think of things that have happened to you. Those are all topics that you can write about in personal narratives.

Try It!

Which of these ideas could you use to write a personal narrative?

Tommy won a race.

A boy climbed a mountain.

I met a new friend.

Take a Look

Nick wants to write about teaching his dog tricks. First he uses a web to write his details in order.

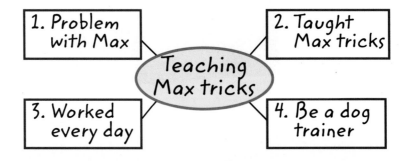

1. Problem with Max

2. Taught Max tricks

Teaching Max tricks

3. Worked every day

4. Be a dog trainer

Student Model

Here's the personal narrative that Nick wrote.

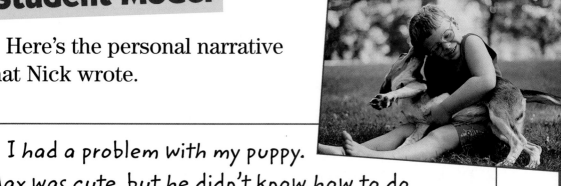

I had a problem with my puppy. Max was cute, but he didn't know how to do much. I wanted him to shake with his paw and fetch a stick. I worked with Max every day after school. I taught him to shake, fetch, and roll over! Max is now a smart dog. Maybe I will be a dog trainer when I get older.

Reading Your Writing

Your personal narrative should be about something that really happened in your life. Make sure you stick to your topic.

Fun Fact

Many people write personal narratives that take up a whole book! These books are a person's own life story. They are called autobiographies.

Tips for Writing a Personal Narrative

Prewriting Make a Plan

▶ Make a list of things that have happened to you lately.

▶ Pick one idea from your list for your topic.

▶ Make a web to organize your ideas.

Drafting Put Your Thoughts on Paper

▶ Write your personal narrative. Use your web.

▶ Don't worry about mistakes. You can correct them later.

Revising Be Sure It Makes Sense

▶ **Ideas** Is it something that really happened to you?

▶ Is it something of interest to someone else?

▶ **Organization** Do you tell the events in order?

▶ **Conventions** Check the spelling.

▶ Make sure you capitalized proper nouns.

Publishing Share Your Personal Narrative

▶ **Presentation** Make a neatly typed or written final copy.

▶ Draw pictures to go with your personal narrative.

Picture Books

A **picture book** has words and pictures. The pictures help tell the story. Picture books are made for young children who are learning to read. Adding pictures helps a reader see more about the story.

Try It!

Can you name a picture book you have read?

Take a Look

Rebecca is making a picture book for her brother. First she made a story map for her ideas.

| Characters: Tony and Rich |
| Setting: Tony's room |
| Plot: what to do on a rainy day |
| Beginning: can't play in rain what to do inside |
| Middle: build fort |
| End: play in fort |

Writing a Picture Book

Next she used her notes to write the story.

Rainy Day

Tony and Rich were sad. They wanted to play catch, but it was raining. They sat in Tony's room and tried to think of something to do.

"I know. We can make a fort," said Tony.

"How?" asked Rich.

"We can use cardboard boxes," said Tony. "We can tape the boxes together and draw pictures on them."

The boys got to work. They taped their boxes together and drew on them. When it was done, they went inside it.

"What a great idea!" said Rich.

Adding the Pictures

Rebecca drew three pictures to go with her story.

Tony and Rich were sad. They wanted to play catch, but it was raining. They sat in Tony's room and tried to think of something to do.

"I know. We can make a fort," said Tony.

"How?" asked Rich.

"We can use cardboard boxes," said Tony. "We can tape the boxes together and draw pictures on them."

The boys got to work. They taped their boxes together and drew on them. When the fort was done, they went inside it.

"What a great idea!" said Rich.

Reading Your Writing

When you make a picture book, make sure your pictures match what's going on in the story.

Tips for Making a Picture Book

Prewriting Make a Plan

▶ List topics that interest you or small children.

▶ Pick one idea from your list for your topic.

▶ Plan your story. Use a story map.

Drafting Put Your Thoughts on Paper

▶ Write your story. Use your notes.

▶ Draw pictures that match your story.

Revising Be Sure It Makes Sense

▶ **Ideas** Did you choose an interesting topic?

▶ **Organization** Do you tell the events in order?

▶ Do your pictures match your story?

Editing/Proofreading Look Closely at the Details

▶ **Conventions** Check your spelling.

▶ Make sure you capitalized proper nouns.

Publishing Share Your Story

▶ **Presentation** Make a cover with a picture and title for your story on it.

▶ Read your picture book out loud and show the pictures.

Realistic Stories

A **realistic story** is a made-up story about people or animals that seem real and things that might really happen.

Parts of a Realistic Story

▶ Characters do things that people or animals might do.

▶ Places in the story are real or seem real.

▶ Events in the story could really happen.

▶ A realistic problem is solved.

Try It!

Which of the ideas below could you use to write a realistic story?

▶ A flying frog saves the world.

▶ A boy wins a singing contest.

▶ A dog rides a bike.

Here's the realistic story that Gemma wrote.

The Party

Juanita was worried. She was afraid that nobody would come to her party. She knew her friend Nikki would be there. What if no one else came? She would feel awful.

Juanita looked out the window. She didn't see anyone. She couldn't watch anymore. She went into the kitchen to wait.

Suddenly, the doorbell rang! She opened the door. There were kids on the porch. After a few minutes, more kids came.

Later, Juanita's mom asked her if she had fun. She said she had a great time! She had worried for nothing.

Try It!

What are some ideas for a realistic story?

Reading Your Writing

Remember to make all the characters and events in your story seem real. If Gemma's story had a cartoon character at her party, it would not have been a realistic story.

Tips for Writing a Realistic Story

Prewriting Make a Plan

▶ Make a list of ideas for your story. Choose the one you like the best.

▶ Choose a setting, a problem to be solved, and the characters for your story.

Drafting Put Your Thoughts on Paper

▶ Write your realistic story. Use your notes.

▶ Don't worry about mistakes. You can correct them later.

Revising Be Sure It Makes Sense

▶ **Ideas** Do your characters act real?

▶ Could your setting be a real place?

▶ Could the events in your story really happen?

Editing/Proofreading Look Closely at the Details

▶ **Conventions** Check your spelling errors.

▶ Check to make sure proper names and places start with a capital letter.

Publishing Share Your Story

▶ **Presentation** Make a neatly typed or written final copy.

▶ Draw a picture to go with your story.

Fairy Tales

A **fairy tale** is a story that has make-believe creatures and places. A fairy tale usually has a happy ending.

Parts of a Fairy Tale

Here are some things you may find in a fairy tale.

▶ It usually begins with "Once upon a time."

▶ It takes place in a faraway, made-up place.

▶ It has make-believe characters, such as elves, dragons, and giants.

▶ It may have royal characters, such as kings, queens, princes, and princesses.

▶ Things often happen or appear in threes, such as three wishes.

▶ A problem is solved.

▶ It has a happy ending.

Try It!

Can you think of a fairy tale you have read? Is there one you like best? What about it makes it a fairy tale?

Take a Look

Julie wants to write a fairy tale. She wrote some ideas down in a story map.

Who: a princess

Where: in the woods

Problem to be solved: She is lost.

How problem gets solved: Elf helps her.

Writing a Fairy Tale

Here is the fairy tale Julie wrote using her story map.

The Lost Princess

Beginning ▶
Royalty ▶ Once upon a time, there was a princess named Dorina.

Problem ▶ One day, while Dorina was walking in the woods, she got lost. She sat on a log and thought about what to do.

Make-believe creature ▶ All of a sudden, she heard a voice say, "What's wrong, princess?" She looked up and saw a strange little creature. It was an elf with a long gray beard.

"I'm lost," said Dorina.

The elf said, "Follow me. I will help you."

Problem solved ▶
Happy ending ▶ Dorina followed the elf through the woods. She was glad when she saw her castle. Dorina thanked her new friend. She was happy to be home.

Tips for Writing a Fairy Tale

Prewriting Make a Plan

▶ Make a list of some make-believe places and things.

▶ Think about some make-believe characters to use. Use a story map to plan your fairy tale.

Drafting Put Your Thoughts on Paper

▶ Write your fairy tale. Use your notes.

▶ Don't worry about mistakes. You can correct them later.

Revising Be Sure It Makes Sense

▶ **Ideas** Does your story have parts that make a fairy tale?

▶ **Organization** Does your fairy tale have a problem? Did you solve it?

▶ Does your story have a happy ending?

Editing/Proofreading Look Closely at the Details

▶ **Conventions** Check your spelling.

▶ Capitalize proper nouns and beginnings of sentences.

Publishing Share Your Fairy Tale

▶ **Presentation** Make a neatly typed or written final copy.

Descriptive Writing

Descriptive writing gives a clear picture to your readers. It helps your readers see what you see. It helps them hear what you hear. It helps them feel what you feel. The following lesson will give you tips on writing good descriptions.

Writing Descriptions

Descriptions are words that make a picture in a reader's mind. The pictures can be of people, places, things, or actions. Description words help the reader see, hear, smell, taste, and feel things the writer tells them.

Try It!

Here are some examples of description words. Can you think of some more?

soft sweater   **blue** sky

loud music   **sour** pickle

Take a Look

Jennifer wanted to enter a writing contest. She decided to write a description. First she chose a topic she could write about using description words. Then she used a web to organize her ideas.

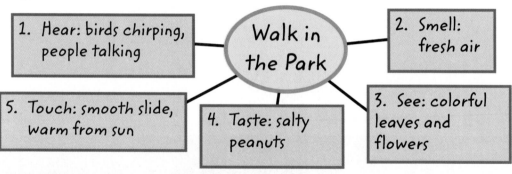

1. Hear: birds chirping, people talking

Walk in the Park

2. Smell: fresh air

3. See: colorful leaves and flowers

4. Taste: salty peanuts

5. Touch: smooth slide, warm from sun

Here's the descriptive paragraph that Jennifer wrote. She used the web to help her.

A Walk in the Park

Mom and I took a walk in the park. We heard birds chirping and people talking. We smelled the fresh air. We saw green leaves and red flowers. We got some peanuts. They tasted salty. At the playground, the slide was smooth and warm from the sun. I love to walk in the park.

Fun Fact

The game "I Spy" is just a describing activity.

Reading Your Writing

Using description words helps your reader better understand your writing. Make sure to use words that help the reader see, hear, feel, smell, or taste things you write about.

Tips for Writing a Description

Prewriting · Make a Plan

▶ List some things you could describe.

▶ Use a web to write details that you can see, hear, smell, taste, or feel.

▶ Pick one idea from your list for your topic.

Drafting · Put Your Thoughts on Paper

▶ Write your description. Use your web.

▶ Don't worry about mistakes. You can correct them later.

Tips for Writing

Revising Be Sure It Makes Sense

▶ **Ideas** Did you choose something that can be described?

▶ **Word Choice** Did you use good describing words?

▶ **Organization** Do you have a topic sentence for your paragraph?

Editing/Proofreading Look Closely at the Details

▶ **Conventions** Did you indent your paragraph?

▶ Did you check your spelling?

▶ Did you use capital letters for proper nouns and the beginnings of sentences?

Publishing Share Your Paragraph

▶ **Presentation** Make a neatly typed or written final copy.

▶ Add drawings or pictures.

Persuasive Writing

Persuasive writing does two things. It can make readers think or feel a certain way. It can also make readers do something. Sometimes persuasive writing can do both of these things at the same time. Advertisements are one kind of persuasive writing.

You will learn about other kinds in the lessons that follow.

Writing to Persuade

One way to persuade your reader to think or act a certain way is to give good reasons.

You can write a persuasive paragraph. First think about what you might want to persuade others to do. That will be your topic. Then write down some reasons.

Take a Look

Jeff wants to persuade his parents to get a dog.

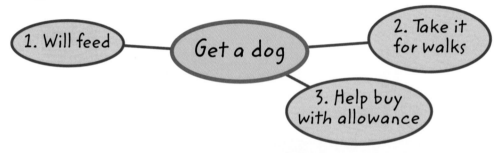

Here's the sample persuasive paragraph that Jeff wrote.

Our family should get a dog. I will offer some of my allowance to help buy one. I will feed it every day. On Saturdays I will take it for a walk. I think a dog would be a good pet for our family.

Reading Your Writing

Make sure you support your topic with good reasons. They will help you show that your topic makes good sense.

Tips for Writing a Persuasive Paragraph

Prewriting Make a Plan

▶ What are some things you want to persuade others to do?

▶ Make a list.

▶ Who will you be trying to persuade?

▶ List some reasons that will persuade your audience.

▶ Put your ideas in a web.

Drafting Put Your Thoughts on Paper

▶ Write your paragraph. Use your web from prewriting.

▶ Don't worry about mistakes. You can correct them later.

Revising Be Sure It Makes Sense

▶ **Ideas** Does your topic persuade others to do something?

▶ Do you have good reasons to support your topic?

▶ **Organization** Did you write your topic in the first sentence?

▶ **Sentence Fluency** Are all your sentences complete? Are they easy to read?

Editing/Proofreading Look Closely at the Details

▶ **Conventions** Check for spelling errors.

▶ Make sure proper names and beginnings of sentences start with a capital letter.

Publishing Share Your Paragraph

▶ **Presentation** Make a neatly typed or written final copy.

▶ Draw a picture to go with your paragraph.

Posters

A **poster** is a big sign. Posters are a way to share information with people. Some posters try to persuade. Posters are often bright and colorful.

Take a Look

Here is a poster Anne made for her school. She wants to persuade others to visit the zoo.

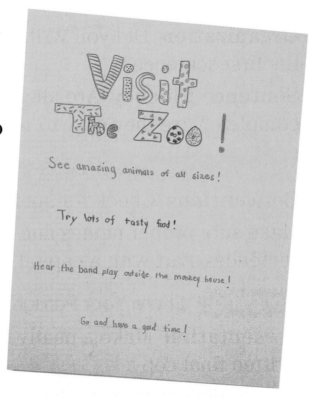

Visit The Zoo!

See amazing animals of all sizes!

Try lots of tasty food!

Hear the band play outside the monkey house!

Go and have a good time!

Try It!

Find the words Anne used in her poster to tell people what they might see, taste, and hear at the zoo.

Posters

Some posters use feelings to tell something. These posters try to get people to think or act a certain way.

Take a Look

Save your paper and, put them in the bins around school.

Help your World ! Recycle

Adam wants his school to recycle. Here is the poster he made for his classmates and teachers.

Reading Your Writing

Making a poster is a great way to share information with others. You can also make a poster to persuade others to do something. Posters are often bright and colorful, so be creative!

Poetry

Poetry is very different from other kinds of writing. Think of some poems you have read. They look very different from stories or articles. There is something else about poetry. It can describe things in a way that you may never have thought about before. The lessons on the following pages will show you how to write some different kinds of poetry.

Rhyming Poetry

Poetry joins the sound and meaning of words to create ideas and feelings.

Poetry is not like other kinds of writing. Below are some examples of what makes poetry special.

▶ Sentences are sometimes broken into parts.

▶ Words that rhyme are often used.

▶ The lines of a poem often have rhythm.

In rhyming poetry the last word in a line rhymes with the last word in another line. Here are some examples of rhyming poetry.

In the example below, the first two lines rhyme, and the last two lines rhyme.

My Best Friend

I have a friend named Sunny.
She makes me laugh. She's funny.
She likes to play board games with me,
And friends we will always be.

More Rhyming Poetry

Here is an example of a poem with three lines. All three lines rhyme.

Flying Balloons
My balloon sailed up in the sky.
It made me say, "Oh my!"
Then it began to fly.

Here is an example of a poem with four lines. Every other line rhymes.

Little Lost Dog
There was a little dog named Star
Who liked to run all day.
But often times he'd run too far
And then he'd lose his way.

Try It!

Can you think of other rhyming words that would fit into the poem above?

Reading Your Writing

Poetry is a great way to entertain your readers. You can write your own rhyming poems with two, three, or four lines.

Nonrhyming Poetry

In **nonrhyming** poetry, the last word in each line does not rhyme. There are many different types of nonrhyming poetry.

Acrostics

Acrostics are poems that use letters of a word or name to begin each line.

Jolly	**S**oft
Exciting	**N**ew
Sweet	**O**utside
Smart	**W**et

Shape Poems

In a **shape poem** words are put together to form a picture. The picture is something in the poem.

My fish is green and red.
He swims
back and
forth.
His name is Fred.

Free-Verse Poems

A **free-verse** poem does not rhyme or have a pattern.

I ride my bike to school.
I see colors on the way.
I love autumn!

Pattern Poetry

Some poetry follows a pattern. Some poems have both length and rhyming patterns. These poems sound like a poem or song you know, but the words are different.

Take a Look

Here is a poem you all know.

Row, row, row your boat
Gently down the stream.
Merrily, merrily, merrily, merrily,
Life is but a dream.

Here is the pattern poem that Alissa wrote using the poem "Row, Row, Row Your Boat."

Ride, ride, ride your bike
Safely down the street.
Carefully, carefully, carefully, carefully,
Bikes are such a treat.

Try It!

Can you think of a short poem or song you like? Try to think of some new words for it.

Reading Your Writing

Pattern poems sound like poems and songs you know. Pattern poems can be fun to write and read. Remember that these poems have the same patterns as other poems, but the words are different.

Structures of Writing

Words, sentences, and paragraphs are the building blocks of writing. Writers use words to build sentences. They use sentences to build paragraphs. You are a writer. You can do it, too.

What Is a Sentence?

A **sentence** expresses a complete thought. It begins with a capital letter and ends with a punctuation mark.

A sentence has a **subject** and a **predicate.** A **subject** tells *what* or *whom* the sentence is about. A **predicate** tells what the subject *is* or *does.*

Take a Look

Turtles crawl.

Turtles is the subject.
Crawl is the predicate.

Try It!

Can you pick out the subject and predicate in this sentence?
Whales swim.

More About Predicates

A predicate can sometimes be just one word. This word is the verb, or action word.

Take a Look

Frogs **jump.**
Birds **fly.**

These sentences have only one word in the predicate.

A predicate can sometimes have many words.

Take a Look

Frogs **jump on lily pads.**
Birds **fly over the ocean.**

These sentences have several words in the predicate.

Reading Your Writing

A subject and predicate are the two main parts of a sentence.

Sentence Problems

A fragment is not a sentence. Something is missing. Sometimes a subject is missing. Other times, the predicate is missing.

Fragment: Won the soccer game.
Sentence: We won the soccer game.

Fragment: My friend.
Sentence: My friend lives near the school.

Run-On Sentences

A **run-on sentence** is two or more sentences run together.

This is a run-on sentence:

Sara studied all night she got an A on her test.

There are two ways to fix the run-on sentence.

1. Sara studied all night. She got an A on her test.
2. Sara studied all night, and she got an A on her test.

Rambling Sentences

A **rambling sentence** has too many sentences, which are usually joined by *and*.

Take a Look

Rambling: We went out to dinner and then we went to the movies and then we went home.

Correct: We went out to dinner and to the movies. Then we went home.

Try It!

How can this fragment be fixed to make it a sentence?

To help my sister.

Fun Fact

Pencils have been used for a very long time, but pencils with erasers weren't invented until 1858.

Reading Your Writing

Fragments, run-on sentences, and rambling sentences are problems for writers and readers. Check your sentences carefully.

Kinds of Sentences

A **declarative** sentence tells something. It ends with a period (.).

George Washington was the first U.S. President.

An **interrogative** sentence asks something. It ends with a question mark (?).

How was your history test?

An **exclamatory** sentence shows strong feeling about something. It ends with an exclamation point (!).

Wow, that is a huge spider!

More Kinds of Sentences

An **imperative** sentence gives a command. It ends with a period (.).

Look at this brown spider.

Try It!

What kind of sentences are these?
    What time is it?
    Close the door, please.
    Dogs bark, jump, and play.

Reading Your Writing

Use different types of sentences when you write. You can use declarative, interrogative, exclamatory, or imperative sentences. Be sure to use the correct end mark.

Paragraphs

A **paragraph** is a group of sentences that tell about the same thing.

Rules for Writing Paragraphs

▶ A paragraph begins on a new line.
▶ The first line is indented.

Topic Sentences

Many paragraphs have a **topic sentence.** It tells the main idea of a paragraph. A strong topic sentence grabs a reader's interest.

Tips for Writing Good Topic Sentences

▶ A topic sentence gives the main idea of the paragraph.
▶ Put the topic sentence at the beginning of the paragraph to let readers know what they are about to read.

Staying on the Topic

All the sentences in a paragraph should work together. Using sentences that don't fit might confuse readers.

Take a Look

Here's a paragraph Mark wrote. He crossed out the sentence that does not stay on the topic.

There is a great new park on our block. It has swings and jungle gyms with slides. It also has sports fields. My sister and I play soccer and baseball there. There is a big pool in the middle of the park. ~~I learned to swim at the YMCA.~~ I like to swim in it with my friends. I have so much fun at the new park. I will spend all my summers there.

Types of Paragraphs

There are many reasons to write a paragraph. You can write a paragraph that

▶ tells a story

▶ explains how to do something

▶ describes something

▶ persuades someone to do something

Try It!

What type of paragraph best fits with each of the following ideas?

▶ trying to get others to recycle

▶ telling a friend about your birthday present

▶ giving directions to your local library

▶ sharing a dream you had last night

Paragraphs That Tell a Story

You can write a paragraph that tells a story. These paragraphs have a beginning, a middle, and an end.

Take a Look

Here's a paragraph that Alex wrote. It is a paragraph that tells a story.

I'll never forget my first day of school. ◀ **Beginning**
I was so scared. I didn't know anyone. I sat
in the back row of my classroom. The kid
in front of me turned around and asked ◀ **Middle**
me my name. His name is Josh. We ate
lunch together that day. We have been
friends ever since. My first day of school ◀ **End**
turned out great.

Paragraphs That Persuade

You can write a paragraph to persuade. You try to make your readers think, feel, or act a certain way. These paragraphs give reasons that support the topic.

Take a Look

Here's a paragraph that Ming wrote. This is a paragraph that persuades.

Reason 1 ▶   Why should I have a pet turtle? Caring for a turtle won't cost much. I could keep my turtle in a cardboard box. Turtles eat lettuce and bugs, so it won't cost much to feed it. Turtles are

Reason 2 ▶   quiet, so my turtle wouldn't bother my

Reason 3 ▶   family. They don't make much of a mess. A turtle is a great pet because it's cheap, quiet, and not messy.

Paragraphs That Describe

You can write a paragraph that describes, or tells, about something. These paragraphs make a picture for the readers.

Take a Look

Here's a paragraph that Seth wrote. It is a paragraph that describes.

My tree house is great. It was built in a huge oak tree. There is a hanging ladder that I use to climb into it. It has one room with four chairs and a card table. I put posters of famous ball players on the walls. There are two windows on either side of the tree house. My tree house is a great place to hang out with friends.

Paragraphs That Explain

You can write a paragraph to give directions or tell how to do something. These paragraphs sometimes have **transition words** in them.

Transition words tell the order of things. Some examples are *first*, *next*, *then*, and *finally*.

Take a Look

Here's a paragraph that Brad wrote. This paragraph tells how to do something.

> Anyone can have a lemonade stand. It's easy. First make a big pitcher of lemonade. Next set up a table in front of your house. Then put up a sign that reads, "Lemonade Sale." Finally bring your pitcher of lemonade and some paper cups to your stand. Now wait for your customers.

Try It!

What are the transition words in Brad's paragraph?

Reading Your Writing

You write paragraphs for different reasons. You can tell a story or describe something. You can explain how to do something, or you can write to persuade.

Fun Fact

Cookbooks have paragraphs that tell how to cook food.

Graphic Organizers

Graphic organizers are tools that help you plan your writing. They come in different shapes and sizes. *Graphic* means "written or drawn." *Organizer* means "tool for getting your ideas in order."

Webs

Some graphic organizers help you gather ideas to describe something.

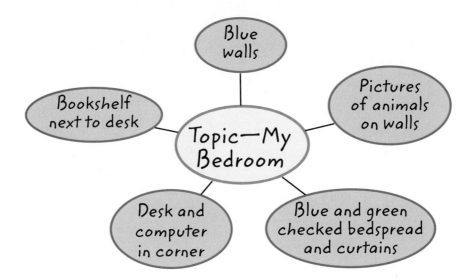

Story Map

Some graphic organizers help you plan a story.

Title	The Poetry Paper

Character	Tonya

Setting	Woods

Plot   Tonya has to write a poem for English.

- Beginning   Tonya can't think of anything to write.

- Middle   Tonya walks in woods instead of writing poem. She sees all kinds of creatures.

- End   Tonya writes poem about things she sees in woods.

Venn Diagram

Some graphic organizers help you compare things.

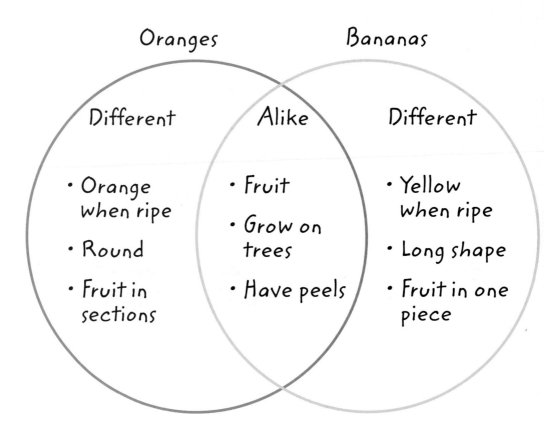

Oranges   Bananas

Different   **Alike**   **Different**

- Orange when ripe
- Round
- Fruit in sections

- Fruit
- Grow on trees
- Have peels

- Yellow when ripe
- Long shape
- Fruit in one piece

Reading Your Writing

Make a plan before you start writing. It is helpful to collect your ideas in a graphic organizer. When you make a plan, readers will better understand what you write.

Writer's Craft

People read what you write. You want them to enjoy your letters, stories, and poems. You want them to learn from your reports and descriptions. You can help them. Here are some ways to make your writing better.

Audience and Purpose

There are two important questions to ask yourself before you begin any writing.

1. Who will read my writing?
2. What is my reason for writing?

The answers will help you to plan your writing in a clear way.

Audience

Your audience is who you think will read your writing. Knowing your audience helps you think about what your readers want to know.

Purpose

The reason you are writing is your purpose. There are four main purposes for writing.

1. inform or tell about something
2. explain or tell how to do something
3. entertain or amuse
4. persuade people to think or do something

Writing to Inform

When you are writing to inform, you are giving information about a subject. It's important to think about your audience. What might your audience already know? What does your audience need to know?

Take a Look

Matlin wrote about the first airplane flight.

The First Flight

On December 17, 1903, Wilbur and Orville Wright flew an airplane in Kitty Hawk, North Carolina. The plane stayed in the air for twelve seconds. The plane flew about 118 feet. The brothers had been trying to fly since 1896.

Writing to Explain

Another purpose for writing is to explain how to make or do something, or how something works. Think about your audience. How much do you need to explain? Be sure to include all the information your audience needs.

Take a Look

Cortland wrote about how to wash the dishes. His audience was his classmates.

	How to Wash Dishes
	1. Fill the sink with hot, soapy water.
	2. Get a clean dishcloth.
	3. Wash and rinse the glasses first.
	4. Wash and rinse the silverware next.
	5. Then wash the plates.
	6. Wash and rinse the greasy pots and pans last.
	7. Put everything in a rack to dry, or dry with a towel.

Writing to Entertain

When you write to entertain, think about what your readers would enjoy reading or what would amuse them. There are many ways to entertain others.

▶ stories
▶ poems
▶ descriptions
▶ plays
▶ comic strips

Take a Look

Look at Isaac's journal entry.

> A Day in the Life of a Sock
>
> Today, as I was sleeping in the deep, dark drawer of the dresser, Tim yanked me out into the bright morning light. He put me on his VERY cold feet. I was walked on all day. First we went to school. Then we went to a scout meeting. After that, we played in the yard! I really had a busy day!

Writing to Persuade

Writing to persuade is when a writer tries to get readers to think, feel, or act a certain way. You need to know who your audience is and what matters to your audience. Then you can figure out what reasons will persuade them.

Take a Look

Kelly wrote a letter to persuade her principal to let the students visit the zoo.

Dear Ms. Hanson,

Many of the students at this school would like to be able to visit the zoo. There are many reasons this would be a good idea.
1. The zoo makes learning about animals fun.
2. We get to meet other students.
3. All the walking at the zoo is great exercise.

Sincerely,
Kelly

Try It!

Can you think of a topic for each purpose for writing? Who would be your audience for each one?

Reading Your Writing

If you don't think of the purpose and your audience before you plan, your writing will not be as clear as it can be.

Using Time and Order Words

Time words show when events take place.

today	yesterday	tomorrow
last week	Thursday	next day

Take a Look

Cody wrote what he did during his spring vacation. He used time words to make it clear when he did each thing.

Last week was my spring vacation. My family drove to Lake Leland. Monday night we set up the tent by the lake. The next day we went fishing and swimming. On Wednesday it rained all day. On Thursday and Friday we went hiking in the woods. The next day we drove home.

Order Words

Using order words will make your writing clearer to your reader. **Order words** tell exactly in what order things happen.

first	later
next	last
then	finally

Take a Look

Nickoli wrote about her class field trip to the zoo. She used order words to make it clear in what order things happened.

Our trip to the zoo was fun. First we saw the monkeys and gorillas. Next we saw all kinds of bears. Then we ate lunch. Later we saw snakes and lizards. Finally we went home.

Using Place and Location Words

There are many words you can use to make your writing clearer to your readers. Place and location words tell where someone is or where something happens. Using these words will make your writing more specific and will help your readers understand what you write.

Here are some place and location words you might be able to use in your writing.

on	out
in	by
into	behind
near	around
above	under
over	beside
outside	inside

Josh wrote a paragraph about getting lost at the fair.

> Getting lost at the fair is not any fun. Suddenly I turned around, and my parents weren't behind me! I walked into the rides area. I looked inside the horse barn next to the front gate. I looked everywhere. Finally I sat down to rest near the roller coaster. Then I saw my parents by the popcorn stand. I was so happy!

Try It!

How may place and location words did Josh use?

Writing Good Beginnings and Endings

A good beginning and ending will make your writing more interesting to read.

Good Beginnings

A good beginning grabs the readers' attention. Here are four ways to start your writing.

▶ Ask a question that will interest the readers.

What would you do if you found a dinosaur bone in your backyard?

Would you tell someone or would you keep it a secret?

▶ Tell about a problem.

Once there was a king who had a beautiful garden. In his garden there was a tree with twelve golden apples. One day the king counted the apples. One was missing.

More Ways to Write Good Beginnings

▶ Use details that describe sight, sound, smell, taste, or touch.

> Tara walked along the hot, dusty road. Her mouth was dry, and she couldn't stop thinking about ice-cold lemonade.

▶ Use dialogue. (Put the speaker's words in quotation marks.)

> "Jason, don't move!" Tad cried. "There's a spider behind you."
>
> "Well, Tad, don't you move either," Jason said slowly. "There's a large bat hanging over your head."

Good Endings

It's important to have a good ending for whatever you write.

Read the ending from a story about a lost dog named Toby.

Toby walked through the dried leaves to the top of a hill. As he got to the top, he heard voices. They were calling, "Toby! Where are you?"

He looked down the hillside and saw his family. Toby's tail began to wag wildly, and he let out a loud bark. Then he raced down the hill to the people who loved him.

Try It!

Think of something you have written. What kind of beginning did you write? Did your ending tell what happened to your characters?

Reading Your Writing

Your beginning is very important. It gets the audience interested in your story. If your writing doesn't have a good ending, your reader may feel let down and confused.

Staying on the Topic

A good way to stay on the topic, or main idea, is to make a prewriting plan. Make a web or map for your ideas. Then use your prewriting notes while you write.

Take a Look

Carmine wrote a paragraph about farm animals. He wrote a prewriting plan, but he forgot to check it as he was writing.

> Farms can have lots of different kinds of animals. Some farms have cows. Drinking milk is very important to farmers. Some have chickens for their eggs. I like scrambled eggs. Lots of farmers have cats and dogs. Some dogs and cats don't get along very well. A farm can be a home for many different animals.

Try It!

How many places can you find in Carmine's paragraph where he got off the topic?

Take a Look

Carmine revised his writing to make sure it stayed on the topic. Read it and compare it to his first paragraph.

> Farms can have lots of different kinds of animals. Some farms have cows for milk. Some have chickens for eggs. Lots of farms have cats and dogs. A farm can be a home for many different animals.

Reading Your Writing

If you don't stay on the topic, you will confuse your readers. Using a web or map will help you stay on the topic.

Using Dialogue

Talk or conversation between two or more people in a story is called **dialogue**. You can use dialogue to make your characters seem real.

Take a Look

Using the exact words between characters can be more interesting than just telling about a conversation.

> Daniel whispered to Rachel to pass the peas.
>
> "Can you please pass me the peas?" Daniel whispered.

Why Use Dialogue in Your Writing?

Dialogue can show how the characters feel, which makes them seem more real to the readers. Dialogue makes your audience want to keep reading.

How to Write Dialogue

Quotation marks (" ") are used when writing dialogue. Use quotation marks before and after a character's exact words.

Take a Look

Here is a dialogue that Nick wrote.

"Did you like going to the park?" asked Chip.

"Yes, but I wish we stayed longer," said Randy.

"Next time, let's take a picnic," said Chip.

"That sounds great," said Randy.

Try It!

Find the quotation marks and the punctuation used in Nick's story.

Making Comparisons

Writers compare one thing to another to help the reader picture things. When you compare, you show how two things are alike in some way. There are many ways you can compare two things.

Similes

A **simile** compares two unlike things using the words *like* or *as*.

Dyan Sheldon uses similes in her story "The Whale's Song." She compares the size of the whales to the size of mountains. She compares the sound of their voices to the sound of the wind.

In her dreams she saw them, <u>as large as mountains</u> and bluer than the sky. In her dreams she heard them singing, <u>their voices like the wind.</u>

Metaphors

A **metaphor** usually says that one thing is another thing. It does this without using *like* or *as*. What is the snow being compared to in this sentence?

The <u>snow is a soft, thick blanket</u> over the city.

Personification

Personification is a kind of metaphor. Nonhuman things are given qualities or actions of human beings.

The <u>trees danced</u> in the wind.

Try It!

Find the simile in the sentence below.
The sun was like a big orange basketball.

Reading Your Writing

When you use similes, metaphors, and personification, your readers can imagine a picture of what you are writing.

Using the Sounds of Words

Using sounds of words in different ways can make your writing more interesting and colorful. There are many ways to use the sounds of words.

Rhyme

Words that **rhyme** have the same middle and ending sounds but different beginning sounds.

The sun sets across the <u>land</u>,
Flashing like diamonds on the <u>sand</u>.

The butterfly dances from place to <u>place</u>,
Giving its beauty to empty <u>space</u>.

Alliteration

Alliteration is when some of the words in a sentence or line of poetry begin with the same sound.

Peter Piper picked a peck of pickled peppers.

Onomatopoeia

Onomatopoeia is using a word that actually makes the sound you want your readers to hear. *Bang*, *slither*, *crunch*, and *hum* are examples.

> The birds <u>swish</u> through the clear sky.
> Everyone jumped as the balloon went <u>pop</u>!

Try It!

Use each of the words below in a sentence.

buzz   rumble

Repetition

When you repeat words, you can stress ideas. You can also add rhyme to your poems.

> Lullaby, oh Lullaby!
> Flower are closed
> And lambs are sleeping.
> Lullaby, oh Lullaby!
> Stars are up, the moon is peeping;
> —Christina Rosetti

Fun Fact

Author Watty Piper uses repetition in the famous children's book *The Little Engine That Could.* The engine says "I think I can" over and over.

Writing a Story

Think of a story you have really enjoyed. Where and when did it take place? What happened? How did you feel about the characters? What did you like most about the story?

Reading stories can be fun. Writing them can be fun, too. Reading lots of stories can help you when you want to write your own story.

Before you begin to write, you need to ask yourself three main questions:

1. Who will be in my story? These are the **characters.**

2. Where and when will the story take place? This is the **setting.**

3. What will happen in the story? What problem will the characters have? How will they solve it? This is the **plot.**

Characters

Characters are the people, animals or imaginary creatures in a story.

Think about these questions.

1. What do my characters look like?

The more details you give about how your characters look, the easier it will be for your readers to picture them.

2. How will my characters act?

Think about what your characters are like. Are they serious, smart, funny, or mean? You decide and then make them talk and act that way in the story.

Some characters may change how they act as the story changes. If they do change, you need to let your reader know why.

3. How will my characters feel?

Show how they feel through the characters' actions and thoughts.

Setting

The **setting** is when and where the story takes place. Describe the setting near the beginning of your story, so your readers can picture when and where your story is happening.

Think about these questions.

1. When does the story take place?

▶ Be exact: yesterday, ten years ago, twenty years from now, Saturday morning, Wednesday at midnight

2. Where does the story take place?

▶ Be exact: the deserts of Arizona, New York City, the top floor of a building, a baseball field, an old house

▶ A story can change settings as things happen. Make sure you tell the readers when the setting changes.

▶ Use sight, sound, and smell words so your reader will be able to clearly picture the setting of your story.

Plot

The **plot** is what happens in a story. The plot usually has a problem that has to be solved. The plot has three parts: the beginning, the middle, and the end.

> Beginning: The events at the beginning of the story should tell the problem. The characters and setting are also included in the beginning of your story.

> Middle: The characters try to fix the problem during this part. How your story will end is still not told.

> Ending: The problem is solved by the characters. How the problem is solved needs to be clear to the reader.

Before you begin to write, think about these things.

▶ What is the problem?

▶ How will the characters deal with the problem?

▶ How will the problem be solved?

Vocabulary

Each word has its own meaning. Writers carefully choose the words they use. They want words to communicate exactly what they want to say. When that happens, their writing comes alive for readers. You can make the same choices when you write. Learning about different kinds of words will help.

Compound Words

Compound words are two separate words put together to make a single word.

> day + time = daytime
> pan + cake = pancake

Sometimes you can figure out what a compound word means by looking at the words that were joined together.

> book + case = bookcase

The compound word doesn't always have the same meaning as the meanings of the two separate words.

> straw + berry = strawberry
> cart + wheel = cartwheel

Always look up words you don't know in a dictionary or glossary.

Try It!

What word can you add to the word *room* to make a compound word?

Antonyms

An **antonym** is a word that means the opposite of another word. Here are some common antonyms.

easy—hard	full—empty
light—dark	old—new
big—little	win—lose
true—false	hot—cold

Try It!

What is an antonym for the word *happy?*

Writing Connection

Antonyms are words with opposite meanings. Use antonyms to make your writing clear and interesting to the reader.

Synonyms

A word that means the same or almost the same as another word is a **synonym.** For example, *cure* and *heal* mean almost the same thing and are synonyms. Here are a few other examples of synonyms.

story—tale couch—sofa
stop—halt easy—simple

Try It!

Think of some synonyms for the word *nice.*

Writing Connection

Synonyms are words that mean almost the same thing. Instead of using the same words again and again, use synonyms to say things in a new way.

Position Words

Sometimes you need to show place or position in your writing.

Here are some common examples of place or position words.

above	inside	over
below	within	near
around	behind	outside
next to	on	under

Fun Fact

There are more than 30 common position or place words.

Some place words have similar meanings, such as *below*, *beneath*, and *under*.

Try It!

Think of a place word that describes where you are sitting.

Writing Connection

Use words that show place or position in your writing to give readers clear pictures of what you are saying.

Homophones

Words that sound the same but have different spellings and meanings are **homophones.** For example, *blue* and *blew* sound the same, but they have different meanings and spellings. *Blue* is a color and *blew* means "did blow."

Here are some other examples of common homophones.

their/there/they're
Did you see <u>their</u> house?
We hope to see you <u>there</u>.
<u>They're</u> going to come later.

right/write
Turn <u>right</u> at the corner.
Did you <u>write</u> your report?

by/buy
I put the book <u>by</u> the door.
Tam went to <u>buy</u> some carrots.

to/two/too
I went <u>to</u> the store.
I bought <u>two</u> pencils.
I like pencils <u>too</u>.

More Homophones

through/threw
The ball went <u>through</u> the window.
Who <u>threw</u> the ball?

son/sun
Shana's <u>son</u> is my friend.
Will the <u>sun</u> come out today?

your/you're
Sign <u>your</u> name on the line.
Call me if <u>you're</u> going to be late.

Try It!

Can you think of a homophone for the word *won?* Use both words in a sentence.

Writing Connection

Homophones may sound the same, but they have different spellings and meanings. Check your writing to make sure you use the correct spelling of a homophone. Using the wrong homophone will confuse your readers!

Homographs

Homographs are words that are spelled the same way but have different meanings. They may be pronounced either the same way or differently. For example, the homograph *bank* can mean "land along a river" or "a place to keep money."

Other examples of homographs are given below.

fair	I won a prize at the <u>fair</u>. Do you think your grade is <u>fair</u>?
bowl	Do you like to <u>bowl</u>? Put the fruit in the <u>bowl</u>.
left	My <u>left</u> shoe is missing. Only one raisin is <u>left</u> in the box.
match	Dad used a <u>match</u> to light the fire. These two gloves don't <u>match</u>.

More Homographs

mean	Did Chip <u>mean</u> what he said? The dog has a <u>mean</u> bark.
stick	<u>Stick</u> this pin in the map. We stirred the paint with a <u>stick</u>.
pitcher	The juice is in the <u>pitcher</u>. The <u>pitcher</u> threw the ball.
can	<u>Can</u> you tie a bow? Open the <u>can</u> of soup, please.

Try It!

Can you think of at least two meanings for the word *miss?*

Writing Connection

Homographs are spelled the same, but they have different meanings. They might also be pronounced differently. Use the correct words in your writing to say exactly what you mean.

Prefixes

A **prefix** is a word part that is added to the beginning of a base word to make a new word.

Here are some examples of common prefixes and their meanings.

Prefix	Prefix Meaning	Example Words
re-	again	reread, retell, refill
un-	not	unfair, unkind
over-	too much	overjoyed, overdone
mis-	bad, wrong	misspell, mistreat, misplace
pre-	before	preheat, preschool
dis-	not; opposite	disagree, dislike, disappear

Try It!

Think of other words that begin with each of the prefixes given in the chart above.

Suffixes

A **suffix** is a word part that is added to the end of a base word. Adding a suffix changes the meaning of the base word.

Here are some examples of common suffixes and their meanings.

Suffix	Suffix Meaning	Example Words
-ful	full of	joyful, hopeful, careful
-less	without	careless, painless
-est	most	deepest, saddest
-ing	acting or doing	walking, talking, running, writing
-er	one who	painter, teacher, driver
-ly	like	sadly, kindly, softly

Try It!

Think of other words that end with each of the suffixes given in the above chart.

Context Clues

When you come across a word in your reading that you do not know, what do you do? One way to figure out the meaning of a new word is to use context clues. **Context clues** are found in other information near the new word.

How to Use Context Clues

Here are a few ways you can use context clues to figure out the meaning of a new word.

1. Look at other sentences for a definition or explanation of the word.

The human body is an amazing <u>organism</u>. **An organism is any living thing.**

2. Look for a synonym.

Tara looked <u>agitated</u>, **or nervous,** when she gave her speech.

3. Look for an antonym.

The dancer was very <u>graceful</u>, **not clumsy,** as he glided across the stage.

Try It!

Use context clues to figure out the meaning of the underlined word in each sentence below.

▶ An adjective <u>modifies</u>, or describes, a noun or pronoun.

▶ There was an <u>error</u>, or mistake, on my paper.

▶ The cloth was <u>moist</u>, not dry, when he touched it.

Writing Connection

Context clues help readers figure out the meaning of a new word. Context clues can be words or pictures. By adding pictures or definitions to your writing, you are giving your readers context clues.

Adjectives

An **adjective** is a word that describes a person, place, or thing. In your writing, use adjectives that appeal to the reader's five senses.

The Five Senses

Sight

Some adjectives help readers see in their minds what you are describing.

> The <u>gold</u> and <u>orange</u> leaves fell from the tree.
>
> She hugged her <u>chubby, worn</u> teddy bear.

Smell

Some adjectives help the reader imagine a smell that is being described.

> Did you smell the <u>fresh, sweet</u> flowers?
>
> The air was <u>stale</u> in the old cabin.

Sound

Some adjectives help the reader hear what is happening.

> The <u>gurgling</u> water poured out of the faucet.
>
> The swarm of angry, <u>buzzing</u> bees left the hive.

More of the Five Senses

Taste

Some adjectives help the reader imagine how something tastes.

> He sliced the <u>tart, juicy</u> apples for his pie.
> We shared a bag of <u>salty, crunchy</u> peanuts.

Touch

Some adjectives help your reader imagine how an object feels.

> The <u>prickly</u> shrub scraped my legs.
> Tad picked up the <u>slimy</u> frog.

Try It!

Think about your favorite snack. How could you describe it using adjectives that connect to the five senses?

Writing Connection

Adjectives describe nouns and pronouns. Use adjectives to help readers imagine the sight, smell, sound, taste, or touch of something.

Rules of Writing: Grammar, Usage, and Mechanics

You know about rules. When you know and follow the rules of a game, you're better at the game. It's the same with writing. Knowing the rules and following them will make you a better writer.

Grammar

Grammar is about how language is organized. Parts of speech, such as nouns and verbs, are grammar. The names for different parts of a sentence are grammar. Knowing about grammar helps you understand how to build sentences that make sense to your readers.

Nouns

Nouns name something. Nouns name people, places, things, and ideas. For example, think of your school, the things you carry to school, and the people you see there. The words we use for these things are all nouns.

person: woman
place: field
thing: whistle
idea: happiness

Different Kinds of Nouns

Common nouns name general things and groups of things. **Proper nouns** name particular people, places, or things. Proper nouns always begin with a capital letter.

common nouns: dog, girl, road
proper nouns: Patches, Ashley,
             Zigzag Road

Singular nouns name one of something.
Plural nouns name more than one.

singular:	adventure, dish, baby
plural:	adventures, dishes, babies

Some plural nouns are irregular. They are not spelled the way you might think.

singular:	wife, man, foot, child
plural:	wives, men, feet, children

Possessive nouns show ownership. Add an apostrophe-s ('s) to make singular nouns possessive. Add an apostrophe (') to make plural nouns possessive.

Possessive Nouns	
singular possessive:	Eric's bike
plural possessive:	boys' bikes

Pronouns

Pronouns take the place of nouns.

Jenna has a used **bike.**

She really likes **it.**

She and *it* are pronouns.

Pronouns						
I	me	you	he	she	it	him
her	we	us	you	they	them	

Some pronouns are singular and some are plural.

Singular Pronouns	**Plural Pronouns**
I, me	we, us
you	you
he, him	they, them
she, her	
it	

Seth went to the park.
He went to the park. (singular)

Josh called **Max and Jesse.**
Josh called **them.** (plural)

Possessive pronouns show ownership just like possessive nouns do.

The man's home is in Alaska.
His home is in Alaska.

That is Sally's mitt.
That is **her** mitt.

Possessive Pronouns					
my	mine	your	yours	his	her
hers	its	our	ours	their	theirs

Do not use an apostrophe (') with possessive pronouns.

The bear's fur is not brown.
Its fur is not brown.

Try It!

This sentence has three pronouns.
What are they?
    He served it to me.

Verbs

Most **verbs** show action. Think of the things you do. You smile, sleep, read, and play. These words are all action verbs.

Saltwater fish **swim** in the ocean.
Some fish **sleep** with their eyes open.
Some fish **eat** plants.

Linking verbs are special. They can connect parts of a sentence to make it complete. Linking verbs do not show action, but they are still verbs.

Whales **are** mammals.
The whale **is** large.
That whale **was** my favorite.
People **were** happy at the aquarium.

Here are some linking verbs.

Linking Verbs				
am	is	are	was	were

Main and Helping Verbs

The **main verb** in the sentence tells what the subject is or does.

Helping verbs are used with a main verb to tell when something is happening or has happened.

I **am** watching the Olympics.
The athletes **have** trained all year.

Here are some helping verbs.

Helping Verbs						
am	is	was	were	have	has	had

Try It!

What is the helping verb in the sentence below?
Qualified athletes have won gold, silver, and bronze medals.

Adjectives

Adjectives are words that describe nouns or pronouns.

Some adjectives tell how many.

Finally, I have **two** dogs.

Some adjectives tell what kind.

They chase a **black** cat.

Articles

The words *a*, *an*, and *the* are a special kind of adjective called **articles.**

Use *a* before a noun that begins with a consonant sound.

Emma has **a** rabbit.

Use *an* before a noun that begins with a vowel sound.

My rabbit ate **an** apple.

Use *the* with any noun.

The apple is red.

Try It!

Think of two adjectives that describe you.

Adverbs

Adverbs are words that describe verbs by telling how, where, or when.

| We must run **quickly.** | how |

| I like to run **outside.** | where |

| I **always** run with my friends. | when |

Try It!

What are some things you do every day? Try to describe them with adverbs.

Writing Connection

Adverbs describe verbs by telling how, when, or where. If you use adverbs in your writing, your sentences will be more descriptive and clearer.

Conjunctions and Interjections

Conjunctions connect words or groups of words in a sentence.

> Diamonds **and** rubies are types of jewels.
> Diamonds can be in rings **or** necklaces.
> I like diamonds, **but** I don't like rubies.

Conjunctions		
and	or	but

Interjections are words that show strong feelings. Interjections can sometimes stand alone as a sentence.

> **Oh!** Did you see that?
> **Ouch!** That hurt!

Try It!

Can you think of a sentence with a conjunction and an interjection?

Parts of a Sentence

A **sentence** expresses a complete thought. A sentence has two parts: the **subject** and the **predicate.**

Subjects and Predicates

The **subject** is *what* or *whom* the sentence is about.

Rabbits jump.

Rabbits is the subject.

The **predicate** tells what the subject *is* or *does*.

The snake **slithered.**

Slithered is the predicate.

Writing Connection

There are two parts to a sentence. The subject tells who the sentence is about. The predicate tells what the subject is or does.

Complete Sentences

A sentence has a subject and a predicate. A fragment is not a sentence. Something is missing. Sometimes a fragment does not have a subject. Other times it does not have a predicate.

Fragment Ran home.
Sentence Ally ran home.
Fragment The little dog.
Sentence The little dog barked a lot.

Every sentence begins with a capital letter and ends with a period or another end mark. A **run-on sentence** is two or more sentences that run together.

Run-on Julie went camping she didn't like the bugs.
Correct Julie went camping. She didn't like the bugs.

Kinds of Sentences

A **declarative** sentence makes a statement.

The American flag has 13 stripes.

An **interrogative** sentence asks a question.

Can we celebrate the 4th of July every day?

An **imperative** sentence gives directions or a command.

Please wear red, white, and blue to the parade.

An **exclamatory** sentence shows strong feelings.

I love fireworks!

Try It!

Can you change this question to a statement and use all of the same words?
Are you going to the picnic?

Writing Connection

You should try using different kinds of sentences. You can tell or ask something. You can give directions or show strong emotion.

Usage

Usage is about how we use language when we speak and write. For example, the rules of usage tell you when to use *is* and when to use *are*. They tell you when to use *taller* and when to use *tallest*. Learning the rules of usage will help people better understand what you say and what you write.

Verb Tenses

Verbs can show that something is going on in the present.

> Jamie **sees** a deer in her neighborhood.

Verbs can show that something happened in the past.

> Jamie **saw** a deer in her neighborhood.

Verbs can be changed from the present to the past. You can do this by adding *-ed* to the end of some verbs.

> I talk.
>
> I talk**ed.**

Some verbs do not add *-ed* to change from the present to the past. They change in other ways.

> **Present**   I sing.
>
> **Past**   I sang.

Linking Verbs in Present and Past

Linking verbs can also show present and past.

Present
Singular verb The bird **is** small.
Plural verb   The birds **are** small.

Past
Singular verb The bird **was** here.
Plural verb   The birds **were** here.

Try It!

Look back at the sentences about Jamie. How did that verb change from present to past?

Writing Connection

Verbs can show that something is going on in the present or the past. When you are writing, your readers want to know when things happen, so remember to use the correct verb tense, present or past.

Subject/Verb Agreement

A subject and verb must agree in a sentence. That means the correct form of a verb must go with the subject. **Singular** means "one." **Plural** means "more than one."

If the subject is singular, the verb must agree with it.

A plant grows.
The leaf withers.

If the subject is plural, the verb must agree with a plural subject.

The plants grow.
The leaves wither.

Making Verbs Agree

Look at the sentences below. What do you notice about verbs with singular subjects?

These verbs end with an *s*.

The plant needs water.
The leaf dies.

The verbs that go with plural subjects do not end with an *s*.

The plants need water.
The leaves die.

Singular and Plural Subjects and Linking Verbs

Here are the rules for using linking verbs.

▶ Use *is* with singular subjects.
The star **is** far away.

▶ Use *are* with plural subjects.
The stars **are** far away.

▶ Use *has* with singular subjects.
The planet **has** many colors.

▶ Use *have* with plural subjects and the pronoun *I*.
The planets **have** many colors.
I **have** many pictures of the planets.

Try It!

Which sentence has a singular subject? Which sentence has a plural subject? Do the verbs agree with their subjects in both sentences?

The sky has many stars.
Those stars are yellow.

Comparing with Adjectives

An **adjective** describes nouns or pronouns. You can use adjectives to compare.

Most adjectives that compare two nouns or pronouns end in -*er*.

> A tree is **taller** than a bush.

Most adjectives that compare more than two nouns or pronouns end in -*est*.

> The pine tree is the **tallest** tree in the yard.

Some adjectives don't add -*er* or -*est* to compare. Instead, they use *more* and *most*. Use *more* to compare two things. Use *most* to compare more than two things.

> A parrot is **more** beautiful than a robin.

> The parrot is the **most** beautiful bird of all.

Try It!

Make a sentence that compares the seals to whales.

Contractions

A **contraction** puts two words together. Some letters are taken out. An apostrophe (') takes the place of the letters that are taken out.

Here are some common contractions that you use every day as you talk. This is what they look like when they are written.

Common Contractions			
I am	→ I'm	she is	→ she's
I have	→ I've	is not	→ isn't
I will	→ I'll	did not	→ didn't
We are	→ we're	should not	→ shouldn't

Try It!

Look at each pair of sentences. Find the contractions. What letters were taken out?

I will fix the mistake.
I'll fix the mistake.

You did not have to do that.
You didn't have to do that.

Mechanics

The rules of mechanics are very important in writing. How and when to use punctuation marks is part of mechanics. When to use capital letters is part of mechanics. Writers who know and follow these rules make it much easier for readers to understand what they write.

End Marks and Abbreviations

Every sentence must end with a period, a question mark, or an exclamation point. These are all **punctuation marks.**

End a sentence with a period (.) when it tells something.

Hawaii is made of islands.

End a sentence with a question mark (?) when it asks something.

Have you been to the island of Maui?

End a sentence with an exclamation point (!) when it shows strong feeling.

It's such an exciting place!

Other Uses for Periods

▶ Use a period after an abbreviation. An abbreviation is a shortened form of a word.

Mr. Robert Payne   Curly **Rd.**

▶ Use a period after initials.

E. B. White   Mary **A.** Taylor

Commas

A **comma** (,) is another punctuation mark. Commas are most often used to separate things in a sentence.

▶ Use commas in dates between the day and the year.

　　January 31, 2003

▶ Put commas after the greeting and closing in a friendly letter.

　　Dear Jenny,
　　Love,
　　Patty

▶ Use a comma between a city and state in an address.

　　Salt Lake City, Utah

▶ In a list of three or more things, put a comma after each word that comes before *and* or *or*.

　　Elm, oak, and maple are all trees.
　　I don't like spinach, okra, or squash.

▶ In a sentence with someone's exact words, use a comma to separate the quotation from the person who said it.

　　Donna said, "I like dinosaurs!"

Quotation Marks and Underlining

Quotation marks are another type of punctuation. They are used in many ways.

Use quotation marks before and after a speaker's exact words.

> Zack said, "I will play my tuba in the gymnasium."

Use quotation marks for titles of stories, songs, and poems.

> Sue just read the story "The Kite in Flight."

Underlining is a way to identify titles of books, plays, and magazines.

> Have you read <u>Ryan's Red Room</u>?

Writing Connection

Quotation marks and underlining provide special information to readers. Quotation marks signal when someone is speaking. Underlining signals some type of published writing.

Apostrophes and Colons

Apostrophes (') are another type of punctuation mark.

▶ Apostrophes are used to make a contraction.
  I will wash my bike.
  I'll wash my bike.
▶ Apostrophes are also used to show ownership.
  Rosa's bike is blue.

Another type of punctuation is the **colon** (:). Here are some ways that you can use the colon.

▶ Colons are used to introduce a list.
  I need these things from the supermarket: milk, eggs, and bread.
▶ Colons also separate the hour and the minutes when you write the time.
  Will you pick me up at 7:30 p.m?

Writing Connection

Apostrophes are used to make a contraction or to show ownership. Colons are used to introduce a list or when you write the time. Remember to put these punctuation marks where you need them.

Capital Letters

Capital letters are an important part of writing. We use capital letters every time we write sentences. Here are some suggestions to help you use them.

▶ The first word in a sentence always begins with a capital letter.
   My brother likes scrambled eggs.
▶ The word *I* is always a capital letter.
   My dad and **I** will be there.
▶ Names of proper nouns begin with capital letters.
   Rose **H**arris   **G**ill **L**ake
▶ People's titles and initials begin with capital letters.
   Dr. **R**uby **G**oode   **J. A. C**ooper
▶ Words used as names begin with capital letters.
   Mom **D**ad **G**randma **G**randpa
▶ Days, months, and holidays begin with capital letters.
   Thursday **N**ovember **T**hanksgiving

More Places to Use Capital Letters

▶ Cities, states, and countries begin with capital letters.

    Chicago   **I**llinois   **U**nited **S**tates

▶ Titles of books, newspapers, stories, songs, and poems begin with capital letters.

    We sang "**H**appy **B**irthday" to Josh.

    Have you read the book *The Seven Sisters?*

▶ The first word a speaker says begins with a capital letter even if its not the first word in the sentence.

    Emily said, "**M**y brother will be home soon."

▶ The greeting and closing of letters begin with a capital letter.

    Dear Sammy,   **Y**our friend,
                             Eddie

Writing Connection

There are many reasons to use capital letters. Remember to check for them in your writing.

Glossary

A

adjective   a word that describes a noun or pronoun

adverb   a word that describes a verb by telling how, when, or where

antonym   a word that means the opposite, or almost the opposite, of another word

apostrophe (')   a punctuation mark used with possessive nouns to show ownership and with contractions to show where letters have been left out

audience   the person or people who read what you write

C

characters   the people or animals in a story

colon (:)   a punctuation mark used to introduce a list in a sentence. It is also used to separate the hour and the minutes when writing the time.

comma (,)   a punctuation mark used to separate items in a series, in dates, and in cities and states

compound word   two or more words put together to make a new word, such as *daytime*

conferencing   a meeting in which a writer and teacher or other classmate discuss the writing and make suggestions to make it better

conjunction   a word that connects other words or ideas. The words *and, or,* and *but* are conjunctions.

D

declarative sentence   a sentence that makes a statement and ends with a period

dialogue   the talk or conversation between two or more characters in a story or play

drafting   the part of the writing process in which you write a draft, or first try, of what you want to say

E

editing/proofreading   the part of the writing process during which you read your writing to check for mistakes in grammar, spelling, punctuation, and capitalization

exclamation point (!)   a punctuation mark used at the end of an exclamatory sentence or after an interjection

exclamatory sentence   a sentence that shows strong feeling and ends with an exclamation point

F

fairy tale   a story that has make-believe characters and places. A fairy tale usually has a happy ending.

fiction   a story that is made up, or not true

fragment   a group of words that is not a complete thought

free-verse poem   a type of poem that does not rhyme or have a pattern

friendly letter   a letter you write to a friend or relative

G

get-well note   a special note or card you send to someone when he or she is sick

H

homographs   words that are spelled the same way but have different meanings

homophones   words that sound the same but have different spellings and meanings

I

imperative sentence   a sentence that gives a command or makes a request. It can end with a period or an exclamation point.

interjection   a word that shows strong feeling. It can sometimes stand alone as a sentence.

interrogative sentence   a sentence that asks a question and ends with a question mark

invitation   a note or card you send to invite someone to a party

J

journal   a place where you can write about your thoughts and ideas

L

learning log   a type of journal or notebook in which you keep a record of what you learned about something

M

metaphor   a comparison of two unlike things without using *like* or *as:* The grass was a soft, green carpet.

N

nonfiction   writing that is about real people, situations, or events

noun   a word that names a person, place, or thing

O

onomatopoeia   using a word that imitates the sound it describes, such as *swish* and *pop*

order words   words that tell in what order things happen, such as *first, next,* and *last*

organization   the way writing is put together, including a good opening, correct order, and an interesting ending

P

paragraph   a group of sentences about one idea

period (.)   a type of punctuation mark found at the end of statements and after abbreviations and initials

personal narrative   a form of writing in which the writer tells something that has really happened in his or her own life

personification   describing nonhuman things as if they were human. The old car *coughed* and *sputtered.*

persuade   to try to get someone to think in a certain way or do a certain thing

picture book   a book in which the pictures are as important as the words in telling the story

play   a true or make-believe story that is acted out for an audience

plot   the action or events in a story. Often, the plot tells about a problem and how it is solved.

plural   more than one

poetry   a type of writing that joins the sound and meaning of words to create ideas and feelings

portfolio   a place to keep your finished and unfinished writing. You can also keep writing ideas and word lists in your portfolio.

position words   words that show place or location, such as *under* and *over*

poster   a big sign used to share information with others

prefix   a word part that is added to the beginning of a base word to make a new word

presentation   the way your writing looks when you are ready to publish

prewriting   a part of the writing process. During prewriting, you choose a topic, gather ideas, and make a plan.

pronoun   a word that takes the place of a noun

proofreading marks   marks that are used when proofreading someone's writing

publishing   the part of the writing process in which you share your writing

purpose   your reason for writing. The purpose could be to entertain, to inform, or to persuade.

Q

question mark   a punctuation mark used at the end of sentences that ask questions

quotation marks   punctuation marks used to show the exact words a speaker says. They are also used for titles of stories and poems.

R

realistic story   a made-up story with characters who seem real and a plot with events that could really happen

report   a piece of writing that gives information about a specific topic

revising   a part of the writing process in which you make changes to improve what you have written

rhyme   repeating syllables that sound alike, such as at the ends of lines of poetry

S

sentence   a group of words that expresses a complete thought

setting   the time and place of a story

simile   compares two unlike things using the words *like* or *as*. The snow was like a white blanket on the ground.

singular   one

suffix   a word part that is added to the end of a base word to make a new word

summary   writing that tells the main idea and main points of a longer piece of writing

synonym   a word that means the same, or almost the same, as another word

T

thank-you note   a note or card you send to someone to thank them for a gift or for doing something special for you

time line   a graphic organizer that shows events that have happened in the correct order

time words   words that show when events take place, such as *today*, *tomorrow*, and *yesterday*

topic   a subject one chooses to write about

topic sentence   a sentence that tells the main idea of a paragraph. Topic sentences most often occur in expository or persuasive writing.

V

verb   a word that shows action or state of being

W

writing process   a plan to follow when writing. The steps are prewriting, drafting, revising, editing/proofreading, and publishing.

Index

The **index** is a list of words and page numbers. It lists the different things that are in the Handbook. The words are in alphabetical order. You look in the list for the word you want to find. Then you look at the page number of the Handbook where it can be found. The index is a good tool. Learn to use it. It can save you a lot of time.

V

Venn diagram, 160
verb, 145, 214–215, 224–227
verb tenses, 224–225
vocabulary, 190–205
    adjectives, 204–205
    antonyms, 193
    compound words, 192
    context clues, 202–203
    homographs, 198–199
    homophones, 196–197
    position words, 195
    prefixes, 200
    suffixes, 201
    synonyms, 194
voice, 12, 15, 30, 77, 92

W

webs, 26, 95–96, 102, 158
word choice, 13, 15, 30, 86–87, 98, 125
writer, 8–11, 35
writing directions, 82–87
writing portfolio, 46–47
writing process, 20–53
    drafting, 20, 28–29, 49, 71, 77, 86–87, 92–93, 98, 105, 111, 115, 119, 124, 130
    editing, 21, 38–41, 52, 71, 77, 86–87, 92–93, 99, 104, 111, 115, 119, 125, 131
    prewriting, 20, 22–27, 29, 48, 71, 77, 86–87, 92–93, 98, 104, 111, 115, 119, 124, 130, 178
    publishing, 21, 42–45, 53, 71, 77, 86–87, 92–93, 99, 105, 111, 115, 119, 125, 131
    revising, 21, 30–37, 51, 71, 77, 86–87, 92–93, 98, 104, 111, 115, 119, 125, 131